THE EMPOWERED CREATOR

Embody the Divine Artist Within YOU!

Katy Speziale

THE EMPOWERED CREATOR: Embody the Divine Artist Within YOU!
www.EmpoweredCreatorBook.com
Copyright © 2023 Katy Speziale

Paperback ISBN: 978-1-77277-530-3

All rights reserved. No portion of this book may be reproduced mechanically, electronically, or by any other means, including photocopying, without permission of the author except in the case of brief quotations embodied in critical articles and reviews. It is illegal to copy this book, post it to a website, or distribute it by any other means without permission from the author.

References to internet websites (URLs) were accurate at the time of writing. Authors and the publishers are not responsible for URLs that may have expired or changed since the manuscript was prepared.

Limits of Liability and Disclaimer of Warranty
The author and publisher shall not be liable for your misuse of the enclosed material. This book is strictly for informational and educational purposes only.

Warning – Disclaimer
The purpose of this book is to educate and entertain. The author and/or publisher do not guarantee that anyone following these techniques, suggestions, tips, ideas, or strategies will become successful. The author and/or publisher shall have neither liability nor responsibility to anyone with respect to any loss or damage caused, or alleged to be caused, directly or indirectly by the information contained in this book.

Publisher
10-10-10 Publishing
Markham, ON Canada

Printed in Canada and the United States of America

I dedicate this book to you, the artist of your life, and your canvas. May you forever be empowered to be your divine self and create so much beauty in the world. You are incredibly powerful and amazing; always remember that!

I dedicate this book to my beautiful niece, Natalie (6). One day you will understand this book, but for now, always remember to be your own person. Be who you are and shine your creative light in this world. There is no one else like you; you are one of a kind! I know you'll create so many beautiful things within your lifetime. I love you!

Table of Contents

Endorsements vii
Acknowledgements ix
Foreword xiii

Chapter 1: What Will You Discover in the Pages Ahead? ... 1
Why I Wrote This Incredible Book for You 3
Katy's 4 I's Framework 4

Chapter 2: Imagination 9
Everyone Has a Beautiful Imagination 11
Mental Images 13
Biggest Consideration 15
Open Your Mind 17
Divinely Be Intentional 20
You Are Powerful 22
Truly Define Your Purpose 24
Harmony 28
Effectively Utilize to the Fullest 31

Chapter 3: Inspiration 35
Develop the Belief of Endless Possibilities 37
Ideas to Feel Inspired 39
Value the Moments and Be Present 41
In a State of Flow 44
Naturally Think Outside the Box 46
Elevate by Trying Something New 48

Chapter 4: Intuition **53**
Awaken Your Intuition 55
Resonate and Follow Your Heart 58
Take Inspired and Aligned Actions 60
Initiate Letting Go of Perfectionism 62
Stop and Know When It's Complete 65
To Go Against the Grain 68

Chapter 5: Ignite **71**
Wonderfully Authentic 73
Infinite Bravery and Boldness 75
Time to Believe in Yourself 78
Have Your Own Ideas 81
Incredible Emotions 84
Now Be Grateful for You 88
Your Style 90
Opportunities 92
Unwavering Faith 94

Chapter 6: A Few Final Thoughts! **99**
Did You See What I Did There? 101
Congratulations 102

Gold Nuggets Recap 103
Your Gold Nuggets 109
Resources 113
About the Author 115

ENDORSEMENTS

"*The Empowered Creator* is the perfect book for any artist and creator who is looking to discover their voice and find their path, as they are figuring out how to create based on who they truly are. Katy delivers the concepts of what the greatest creators have done to achieve their greatness, and explains how you can take the same principles and incorporate them into your everyday practice.

Creators are meant to think big. They've been given a gift to make this world such a beautiful place, and in this book, Katy beautifully gives you the tools you need to take your work and your life to the next level, so you too can achieve extraordinary things. I've intuitively used the process she describes throughout my entire career."

- **Samantha Kaplan – artist, entrepreneur, thought leader**

"If you care deeply about finding your purpose and are seeking long-term happiness in your life, be sure to put this book on your required reading list. In this beautiful informative guide, you will learn to empower yourself, eliminate excuses, and learn to speak (and live) your truth. Katy's inspiring guidance and wisdom will provide the boost you need to be an empowered creator of your dream life."

- **Tiffany Neuman – founder of Your Legacy Brand**

For bonuses go to www.EmpoweredCreatorBook.com

"I love how Katy helps you discover the power within yourself. As a full-time artist, I find her book is a useful tool to help motivate and empower myself; there is a lot of wisdom and guidance. Thank you Katy!"

- **Noemie L. Cote – Canadian landscape painter**

"*The Empowered Creator* is an amazing book that is loaded with knowledge. It is straight to the point and easy to read. Katy is passionate and puts her heart and soul into everything that she does, which is demonstrated in her book and her art."

- **Samantha Joseph Hinds – beauty brand creator, speaker, life coach**

ACKNOWLEDGEMENTS

Thank you, **Douglas Hunt,** for being my first mentor for my art, and my first inspiration that it's possible to write a book! After I saw your biography book at a fair, it made me want to write a book about my artwork one day. My plans changed on the topic of my book, but that was the first moment that I felt inspired to write a book.

I would like to thank **Amy Deschenes** for being a supportive leader and for inviting me to that personal development training that literally changed the course of my life. Thank you for all that you do!

Thank you so much to **Kathleen Cameron** for doing an "Ignite your Calling" training in July 2021. That training introduced me to a new way of thinking and the world of personal development. Your training made me realize that my calling is my art, and that it always has been and always will be. I had always kept it on the side, but now I know without a shadow of a doubt that I am meant to create and bring so much colour, inspiration, and joy to the world. Thank you for impacting my life! I am truly grateful.

For bonuses go to ...

Thank you, **Kathryn Ingle,** for supporting me at the beginning of my personal development journey. I appreciated your support and guidance.

Thank you to the late **Bob Proctor** for inspiring me to think. Thank you for inspiring me to be courageous and to not be afraid to be who I am. Your way of life and guidance are forever appreciated.

Thank you, **Susanne Bambrauch,** for taking the time out of your day to virtually meet with me. Thank you for introducing me to Samantha. You led me to the next steps to take on my artist journey, and I appreciate that wholeheartedly.

Thank you, **Samantha Kaplan,** for guiding me to become more self-aware of who I am and to become aware of my goals. My consciousness has grown so much! Thank you for being my mentor; I appreciate all that you do. Thank you for moving me into action and for encouraging me to reach my goals.

I'd love to thank my grandma, **Georgette Cebrario,** for showing me that publishing a book is possible for anyone. My exact thoughts are, "If Gram can do it, so can I!" Thanks for your inspiration. Love you!

Thank you to **Tiffany Neuman**, for guiding me through your Legacy Brand Foundations Program. Your branding process wasn't just about branding; it was a whole self-discovery process in my eyes. I learned so much about myself and about who I want to help, which brought me to what I wanted my book to be about. You have truly helped me find myself as a person, and I highly thank you for that and for everything else you helped me with on my journey. I'm forever grateful.

Thank you to my publisher, **Raymond Aaron,** for guiding me through the book writing process in the most effortless and easy way. I appreciate your knowledge in the field. Thank you for publishing my book!

I'd love to thank **Barbara Powers**, my book architect, for guiding, supporting, and encouraging me through my book writing journey. You have been there for me every step of the way, and I appreciate all that you've done for me. I'm grateful to have you in my life.

Thank you to **Liz Ventrella, Waqas Chaudhry,** and **Lisa Browning**, for helping with the creation of my book. I appreciate your time and help.

Thank you, **Mom and Dad,** for supporting and encouraging my creative and artistic passion throughout my life. I love you!

FOREWORD

Do you think of yourself as creative? Have you found your calling in this life? Do you believe that you are doing what you are meant to be doing?

If the answer to any of these questions is no, *The Empowered Creator* is the book for you!

When I first met Katy Speziale, the first things that I noticed were her creativity, intelligence, and determination. She is an incredibly talented artist and a well-deserving award-winning author.

While reading *The Empowered Creator*, I could see that it came straight from Katy's heart and soul. I could feel her powerful energy exuding through the pages, and I am confident that you will as well. I appreciate how she utilizes her imagination to the fullest, as well as her ability and intention to empower you through this book.

Through these pages, you will:

- Overcome the trap of perfectionism
- Develop confidence in your abilities
- Discover your creative side

For bonuses go to www.EmpoweredCreatorBook.com

With Katy's 4 I's Framework (Imagination, Inspiration, Intuition, and Ignite) you too will become an Empowered Creator. I wish you well on your journey!

Raymond Aaron
New York Times **Bestselling Author**

CHAPTER 1

What Will You Discover in the Pages Ahead?

*"Passion is energy. Feel the power
that comes from focusing on what excites you."*
– American talk show host, Oprah Winfrey

Why I Wrote This Incredible Book for You

So, why did I write this book? Well, it all started with an online personal development training that I was invited to back in July 2021, called "Ignite Your Calling," by Kathleen Cameron. As I was doing the questions in the workbook for the 5-day training course, all the questions kept leading me back to my art. I kept trying to resist and push those thoughts away to stick with answers that made sense for the job I was doing at the time. No matter how hard I tried to resist, my art just kept being pulled back into my mind. I ignored that for a while.

I started taking more online personal development courses, started to read, etc. It's funny because, before that, the only thing that I read was cookbooks. I finally found a topic I thoroughly enjoy reading about! I love to learn, grow, and expand my consciousness.

Eventually, I began to realize that the job I was doing at the time wasn't what I was meant to be doing. My purpose is so much bigger than that! My passion is art! I have been painting with acrylics on canvas for over 14 years and love every moment of it. Painting brings me so much peace and happiness and I absolutely love bringing a piece of happiness to homes. I am an artist, and I am meant to bring so much colour and inspiration to the world.

When it came to things like coming up with my own ideas as an artist, I realized that I was an unconscious competent. I was coming up with lots of ideas but didn't exactly know how I was doing it. Throughout more courses I became aware of the how, which I will talk about soon enough.

I joined another online course, which allowed me to begin thinking bigger. While thinking of what I would love to do with my life, I realized that I've always wanted to write a book, and it suddenly hit me what I would like to write the book about. I knew I wanted to help people overcome certain aspects of their lives, build confidence, etc. It's funny, though, because my idea for my book title was a lot different from the title now. A lot changed through my personal growth and development journey.

I took the Legacy Brand Foundations Program with branding expert, Tiffany Neuman, and this is where my 4 I's Framework came to life. You will hear more about that framework right now!

Katy's 4 I's Framework

Within these next chapters, you will become more aware of the power within you, push past perfection, push past social standards, see "mistakes" as beautiful opportunities, and so much more. You will develop confidence, bravery, faith, and unravel the divine artist within you. You already know you're an artist, so it's time to fully embody the divine artist within YOU! Step into and be the ultimately incredible artist you're destined to be. You are the creator of your life and your canvas; it's time to step into that power!

I have created my 4 I's Framework, which will help you spark your divine self and release the empowered creator within you. This is the exact formula I use to create my art, and it gives me endless original ideas, a positive mindset, confidence, bravery, and ultimately, empowerment. The 4 I's are: Imagination, Inspiration, Intuition, and Ignite.

I became aware of everything that I pushed through as an artist, and as a person. I'm so honoured, grateful, and excited to share my framework with you so that you can push past your barriers as well, to bring out the divine artist within you!

I was personally a huge perfectionist in high school, and I know how exhausting and limiting it can feel when you're trying so hard to make everything absolutely perfect (in your eyes). Being on the other side now, there's less pressure, and my art is imperfectly perfect; it's wonderful to feel this way! A change in mindset is all it is!

I also know how frustrating it can feel to not know how to come up with your own ideas in art, and I also know how magical it is to come up with my own beautiful ideas now, with ease and flow. In high school, when my art teacher would tell us to come up with our own ideas for an assignment, I wouldn't know what to do. I had no idea where to even begin to produce my own ideas at that point in my life. I'm so grateful that I know how to now, so that I can share with you.

I definitely understand how defeating and upsetting it can feel to make a "mistake" in your art. It is wonderful to overcome this and see any smudge or "mistake" as a beautiful opportunity. In art class, when my paintbrush used to accidentally hit the wrong spot on the canvas, it felt so defeating. I've had this happen several times over the years as an artist and truly see it as a blessing in disguise now. I'd love for you to feel the same.

This book will help you push past all these moments of doubt and fear so that you can soar into being the empowered creator that's already within you! Have you ever heard that success is only 5% strategy and 95% mindset? Well, it's time to build bravery, boldness, and confidence within you!

Warning: You may have some realizations from this book—some "aha" moments. Some may be hard to swallow, but they're good. It's good to be aware of yourself so that you can decide to change and grow. This book might be an entirely new perspective for you to hear. In that case, I hope it opens your eyes to a new way of being. It may challenge some of your underlying beliefs and past thinking. I know that everything that I've learned through my personal development journey completely challenged my way of thinking. It feels so good to be free! I choose what I want my beliefs to be.

While reading, I invite you to take an honest look at yourself. When I say an honest look, I don't mean with judgement or disappointment; I mean staying neutral but taking a truthful look to see the areas in your life where you can expand and grow. See it as an opportunity for growth within yourself. As you read, I challenge you to keep an open mind about learning new concepts (if you haven't been exposed to this way of thinking before). Here's to becoming more aware and changing from within! Empowerment, here you come! Meet you on the other side!

In the next chapter, you will find out why imagination is incredibly important when it comes to creating your life, and your art. Happy reading!

CHAPTER 2

Imagination

"Imagination is more important than knowledge. Knowledge is limited. Imagination encircles the world."
– Albert Einstein

Everyone Has a Beautiful Imagination

Have you ever thought, "I'm not really that creative." I have heard this exact line from so many people throughout my art journey. Then, these people proceed to tell me who they perceive as creative in their lives. If you've ever thought this, I am here to burst your bubble a little bit and tell you that YOU are creative, and so is everyone else on this planet! And if you haven't thought about it, then bravo to you!

If you have lived on Earth for more than a day, you are a creator. You are always using your beautiful imagination to create with, whether you realize it or not.

Imagination plays such an important role in our everyday lives, and we may not even realize it. This is true on so many levels. Imagination truly is everything! It determines what will be created each day in your life.

So, what is imagination? Imagination is one of your higher faculties of thinking. Unlike your five senses, these higher faculties are what separate you as a human being, from the rest of the animal kingdom. You, as a human, have higher faculties of thinking, such as imagination, intuition, will, perception, etc., and if you choose to use them intentionally, you can truly change your life and the world around you, in so many beautiful ways. Imagination is forming new concepts, ideas, and images in your mind without the input of your 5 senses. It's not something you can hear, taste, touch, or see physically with your eyes, but you can see it in your mind and imagine its realness. Imagination is inventing something new. You can bring something new and exciting to the world!

The amazing thing about the imagination is that it's like a muscle. Keep using it and it will continue to expand and grow. Build the muscle of your imagination! The more you use it, the more ideas will flow to you regularly!

I used to use my imagination in so many different ways and was not aware of any of it. If you have ever had thoughts of, "I hope this doesn't happen," or, "I'd love for this to happen," that is literally your imagination at work, creating potential scenarios and pictures in your mind. You are using your imagination all the time to create your outcomes in life, and you may not even have realized it until now. The good thing is, now that you are aware of this, you can use your imagination in a positive way to create anything you want, in your life and in your art world!

I know you might be thinking, "What does any of this have to do with embodying the divine artist within me?" Well, it's like Albert Einstein's quote: *"Imagination is everything. It is the preview of life's coming attractions."* What you create in your imagination IS that "coming attraction."

Imagination is literally the foundation for everything you do, and for everything that happens in your life! Never take it for granted; your imagination is a true blessing.

So, how exactly does your imagination work? You're about to find out!

Mental Images

The creative process of the imagination works by forming mental images in your mind. Every thought you've had up until now, you've likely thought of an image that goes along with it. For example, if you were to think of a plant, you would likely create a picture in your imagination of a plant. You can probably see one right now because we're talking about it. This is a mental image. It is an image that is not seen through your 5 senses but is in your mind, in your imagination!

I find it really interesting that we used to use our imaginations all the time with ease, when we were children. We would come up with the most amazing new ideas and concepts. What changed? Why aren't we utilizing our imaginations like we did as children? Well, the best explanation that I've heard is that as we grew, outside circumstances may have substantially affected how we utilized our imaginations. For example, if someone has ever said to you, "Stop daydreaming," "Be realistic," or "You can't do that; that's never going to happen," messages like that end up sticking, making a doubtful, negative impression in your subconscious mind; especially when they are said with a lot of intensity from someone you love deeply and look up to, like a parent or family member. This can also take a toll on your self-image, how you perceive yourself. You may have felt judged for utilizing your imagination, and because you felt a deep emotion about the situation, you stopped utilizing it to its fullest potential and power. By not utilizing your imagination consciously, you will unfortunately stay stuck.

It's good to realize certain situations that have happened in the past, like the ones I just mentioned, so that you can let go, release them, and move on since they aren't serving you. How can you move on? Forgive and send love to the people! Even if you don't agree with what they said, you can say in your head, "I don't condone what so-and-so said to me, but I am choosing to forgive him or her." Make the decision to let it go. You are free and an awakened human being!

YOU are creative; YOU can do anything you put your mind to. So, keep dreaming, take aligned actions (actions that are in alignment with your divine self and are based off of your priorities, values, and goals) to reach your dreams, and create the most profoundly incredible artwork that you've ever made in your entire life! As the late Bob Proctor always said, *"If you see it in your mind, you will hold it in your hand."*

Tap into your imagination now, like you did as a child, and don't hold back! Allow it to create the most spectacular images in your mind. Create mental images of what you would love to create, in life and in your art world. Hold the vision and take aligned actions.

Your imagination can truly create anything you want in life, so always remember to consider before you think. Find out in the next section, the biggest consideration you'll want to make when using your imagination.

Biggest Consideration

When using your imagination, please remember this one really big consideration! Here it is: Use your imagination for good, and use it to create a positive impact on the world.

It is so important to use your imagination for good, to make your life more fulfilling and to make the world a better place, every single day.

Now I'm sure you're asking, "Is it possible to use my imagination in a bad way?" The answer is, absolutely! Your imagination is constantly creating scenarios and different situations in your mind. I became aware of that with myself. I would use my imagination to create a situation of worry or fear in my head of what might happen in a particular situation in the future. That's such a negative way to utilize the imagination. I'm so glad I became aware of what I was thinking! Now I catch myself in the act when a negative scenario pops up in my head, and I reframe my thoughts so that my imagination creates with possibility, growth, and happiness, and generates beautiful ideas, paintings, etc. I use my imagination for good and to create best-case scenarios instead.

Let go of what's not serving you! Think about the last time you thought you were going to fail at something. For example, "I am not going to get any sales in my business after Christmas because no one will have the money to buy or will want to buy." That is a preconceived idea and a truly crumby belief to hold! It's basically a self-fulfilling prophecy and I am 100% guilty of doing this in the past. I'm beyond grateful that I now know how to monitor my thoughts to catch myself in that thinking, and to reframe the thinking by changing my mindset. Next time, when you're in a situation like that, switch the situation completely around and imagine, "Wow! My products are going to sell like hot cakes after Christmas, and hundreds of people will be willing and able to purchase them!" It's all about reframing your thoughts in a positive light to attract what you truly want.

As soon as you realize a thought that isn't serving you, be thankful that you became aware of it. Now you can shift the thought to a positive belief that will enhance your growth as an individual. Believe the new belief with whole-hearted faith and hold onto it! Watch how things unfold and change in your life. With feeling and aligned action in the mix, magic will happen! You will consciously manifest your desires!

With all of this being said, be mindful of what you are creating with your imagination; try to be consciously aware and monitor your thoughts. Trust me, I know that at first it will feel absolutely exhausting, and you'll be wondering, "How am I supposed to control even half of the thousands and thousands of thoughts I have on a daily basis?" I know from experience that it may feel overwhelming at first, like very overwhelming, but it does get easier overtime. It eventually becomes more natural.

Now that you know how to use your imagination for good, and to bring positivity into the world, it's time to open your mind to your imagination!

Open Your Mind

Choose to open your mind to your imagination. Your imagination encircles the world and has the ability to create so much beauty and light, so give it a chance to create. You never know what ideas you'll end up coming up with! You'll most likely be pleasantly surprised about what your mind creates when you set it free.

I would love for you to start playing around with the idea of possibility. Open your mind to a world full of possibilities. The possibilities are truly endless! You will hear me say that a lot, but it's so, so true. As long as you are open to seeing the possibility of something different from what you already know, you will allow new ideas and concepts to express themselves within your imagination. How exciting is that!

For bonuses go to ...

Utilize your imagination to its fullest potential and be open to believing its realness. A beautiful quote that I absolutely love is, *"Everything you can imagine is real,"* spoken by Pablo Picasso, a Spanish painter. Everything that you can imagine, you can create. Your imagination creates your reality. What you create in your imagination with a lot of intensity and positive feeling is already created in the spiritual plain, so hold the belief and faith for it to show up in your physical world. Well, it doesn't really just show up I guess; you need to have faith, intense feelings, passion, AND aligned action. Those are all important to ensure that what you create in your mind will inevitably express itself in your physical world. Just never give up.

Be open to not focusing on what you are experiencing in your physical world and, instead, spend time in your imagination, in the 4D (as a lot of people call it). What I mean by this is that your physical world (3D world) is just what you're experiencing at this current moment, and it is happening from thoughts you had in the past. So, if you want different results in the future, think differently! Pull your focus into your imagination and think about what you would love to create. You can create absolutely anything you want! Your 4D world is where all your dreams have already manifested on a spiritual level. Believe that everything you desire has already happened! When you make decisions in your life, think from this spiritual level of already having achieved what you want to achieve. Grow into the person who has already achieved it, and you will manifest it into your 3D world much quicker. Believe it's already yours!

Be willing to tap into the unknown; you don't have to know the "how" of how things will happen, turn out, or how to reach your desire, etc., you just have to know where you want to go and what you want to create! When you have faith in the outcome/goal/destination, you will reach it regardless of what path you take! The "how" will show itself as you take aligned action towards your destination; just keep moving forward. It's like driving to a destination; you can only see so much of the road in front of you, but you have faith that you will still reach your destination if you keep driving! More and more of the road (the how) shows itself as you keep driving.

I truly believe that everything happens for a reason. Remember, when you're allowing your mind to stay open and imagine, the new ideas and concepts that pop into your mind are yours to create, if you choose to take action on them of course. Think about it; you're the one that's imagining that idea for a reason, even if you don't know what the reason may be at the time, so it's likely to eventually show itself. Stay open-minded to different outcomes and possibilities. Be open-minded to any possible way that something can happen! Ideas and concepts will come to you effortlessly if you stay open to receive them!

Now that you are open to your imagination and allowing it to express itself, it's also important to be intentional with your thoughts. Having intention is so important, and you will see why in the next section.

For bonuses go to ...

Divinely Be Intentional

You're probably thinking by now, how much more is there to know about the imagination? Well, the imagination is your most important tool in your mind, so the more you know about it, the better you will understand how it works. The better you understand how it works, the better you will be at utilizing it. Stay with me here! I know some of this may be confusing, but it will all come together in the end and make sense.

Intentionally create what you want in your life and in your artwork. You can create with intention by being mindful. Being mindful means to be consciously aware of what ideas and concepts you are creating. Create thoughts with the intention in your mind of who you want to become. When your thoughts are intentional and in alignment with your divine self, that's when the magic happens. You will generate new ideas with intention. Think about the purpose of why you want to create something; this will form an intention to hold in your thoughts while you're creating new ideas in your mind. The new ideas will then be generated with that intention.

For creating an artistic piece of work such as a painting, think about what concepts and ideas you want to portray through your artwork. Start thinking about the meaning you want the artwork to have. Once you have your meaning in mind, hold the meaning behind the artwork in your mind as you're creating it. This will help you create the piece of art in an intentional way of how you want the artwork to feel when you're done.

You can place an intention of what your artwork means, but remember, it might mean something different to someone else. Everyone's perceptions of art are so different and unique to them, and that's okay. It's actually really beautiful to hear about what people see in your art, how they perceive it. Everyone's feelings towards it will be unique to who they are and to what they've experienced in their lifetime.

For life in general, be intentional with your thoughts by always having your vision in mind. Your vision is what you want to create and what you want your life to look like: basically, how you are living your life at the end goal! A vision is how you see yourself living, the qualities you wish to have as a person, and what you would love to experience in life. If you've never thought about a vision, I highly encourage you to do so. It's nice to know the truth about yourself: who you are and where you're going! Then you're able to hold that vision in your mind while you're taking aligned action towards it. That's using intention… and as American author Wayne Dyer once said, "Our intention creates our reality."

The next section will really tell you the true power of using your imagination. It's time to step into YOUR power!

For bonuses go to ...

You Are Powerful

Everything that has happened in your life is a result of your imagination, your past thinking. With knowing this, you also know that this means you control what you create in your future!

I used to listen to outside sources and never took the time to think about what I want for myself. Not what everyone else wants for me, but what I want for me. Now I know how amazing it feels to know what I truly want in life! I highly encourage you to sit down and push everyone else's thoughts aside and take charge of your imagination—go within! You will be surprised by what you imagine for yourself. Just think, "What would I love? What would I love to create?" Don't let anyone else's opinions come into your mind but your own! Take ownership of who you are so that you can move towards becoming your divine self and embodying the artist within you. Create what's in YOUR heart, not someone else's!

You have the power to create a mental image of something that doesn't even exist in the physical form yet; something that is not yet experienced by your 5 senses. It's a brand-new concept, a brand-new idea; always remember that! You have the power to literally create whatever you want in life, and in your art creations. It's absolutely incredible!

"Passion is energy. Feel the power that comes from focusing on what excites you." This is an amazing quote by American talk show host, Oprah Winfrey. So, what are you passionate about?

You most likely love creating works of art or creations of some sort if you're reading this, but we all have something that we're passionate about that sets our souls on fire (in a good way). We hone in on so much power within us when we focus on our passions and what excites us the most!

Now think about the power your imagination truly holds! Embody the vision you hold in your imagination and become absorbed in it: a healthy obsession some may call it. Make your vision feel more real than what's going on in your physical world. Like we talked about in the section "Open Your Mind," whenever you are thinking of something with true passion and feeling behind it, while taking aligned action towards it, it is sure to manifest in its physical form. Feeling is what truly takes things to the next level; and with a lot of intensity, you will manifest what you want to create, faster!

Tap into your potential; we all have it! We are all made of the same cosmic dust and energy! Our circumstances just vary because of how we choose to use our imaginations on a day-to-day basis. So, what are you manifesting into your life? I recommend choosing by consciously manifesting, a.k.a. being aware of what you are manifesting through your thoughts and actions.

You have the power to control your thoughts! No one has the power to create your world but you. Being aware of this will allow you to step into that power to change the outcome in your life and make it what you truly want it to be.

You have the choice to use your imagination in an amazing way. You are an incredibly powerful being and have so much momentum. Utilize your power and create what you were destined to create. Now that you know how powerful you truly are, it's time to define your purpose!

Truly Define Your Purpose

What is your purpose here on Earth, your purpose for creating what you create, and your purpose for what you want to create in the future? I know that these can feel like huge questions to ask yourself, but they're truly worth asking. Once you figure it out, it will bring so much clarity and peace to your life, by knowing who you truly are inside: your truth!

Defining your purpose as an artist will help inspire you to continue creating every single day. When you discover your purpose here on Earth, that's what will make you want to get up out of bed in the morning. You'll know the reason why you're creating, and that will help you to want to keep going no matter what challenges come your way or arise on your journey. When your purpose is a burning desire within you, there is no stopping you from reaching where you want to go—your end goal! The same thing goes for your life!

Your purpose is what you're truly meant to do during your time on Earth. When I discovered my purpose, it made me feel so whole and happy! I know what I'm here to do, and I'm taking aligned actions to reach my goals every single day. I'm meant to be creating! I am a passionate artist, author, creativity cultivator, imagination catalyst, etc. I am meant to bring so much colour, inspiration, and joy to the world, and I love the impact I am making in the world!

"I have looked in the mirror every single morning and asked myself: 'If today were the last day of my life, would I want to do what I am about to do today?' And whenever the answer has been 'No' for too many days in a row, I know I need to change something," spoken by Steve Jobs, American entrepreneur. I feel that everyone should take the time to find their purpose in life. It is so important to do what you are meant to do in your lifetime, and to feel so fulfilled every single day by doing it!

So, you may be thinking, "How do I find my purpose?" Well, it starts with pushing out everyone else's opinions and perspectives. I mentioned this when we talked about your vision. In my experience, I didn't realize how much my outside circumstances, and the people around me, were truly affecting some of my decisions in my life. Did you hear that? MY LIFE! Yet, I was allowing their opinions and limiting beliefs to create some of my path, and I was choosing to keep myself small. Part of me always knew that there was so much more for me in this lifetime, and you are probably feeling the same way right now (if you don't already know your purpose of course).

Here's what I basically did to figure out my purpose, and you can do it as well! Put yourself in a bubble (metaphorically) and really think about what you want for your life, not what everyone else wants for you. Again, push their thoughts aside; think about what you want for you! Focus on YOU! What do you enjoy doing? What makes you happy? What do you do effortlessly that would probably be more difficult for others to do, but it comes so easily to you? What are your natural talents, abilities, and strengths? What would you love to do? Imagine a different life for yourself, a different way of living. Really allow yourself to imagine all the possibilities that are waiting for you to discover!

Push the thought of money aside as well. That's often an internal block for a lot of us and can hold us back from doing what we're meant to do and reaching our full potential in life. We'll think things like, "I'd love to do this, but I don't have the money," and "I'd love to live life differently, but I don't have enough money." Those are very limiting beliefs to have and can stop you from being who you're meant to be! The only thing in the way of your dreams is you! Why don't you try giving yourself a chance in life instead? What would you love to be doing if money wasn't a factor; or in other words, if you had all the money in the world? Think from that perspective! I bet you would be doing something a lot different than what you are doing right now, and you would probably be impacting the world in a beautiful way. So why aren't you doing what you truly want to do, deep down? See yourself as prosperous and allow yourself to grow and expand. Where there's a will, there's always a way; so believe in yourself!

Take the time to go to a quiet, calming space by yourself and answer some of these questions. "I don't have time, though, Katy," you may be thinking. Well, that's a choice. We all have the choice of what we would like to prioritize and, let me tell you, it's an easy decision for me! Sometimes we need to slow down from our everyday lives and the crazy non-stop routines that we have, and just breathe. Really get in tune with yourself. Just be you! It literally took me two days of just sitting there with myself, in my own energy, to figure out who I am and what I actually want to do with my life—what I'm meant to be doing! Well, actually, I just brushed the surface and dug deeper a few times after that to discover even more about myself. It may take you less time, but it is seriously so worth it to answer these questions and figure out who you truly are!

Your purpose is likely something to do with creating, if you are an artist. If you know you are meant to be creating, the only thing that is stopping you from doing so is you. You are likely stopping yourself because of limiting beliefs you hold, such as fear of success, fear of being seen, fear of failure, fear of being different and being judged, anxiety and disbelief in yourself, and people telling you that "artists can't make money," and you choose to hold that as a belief and don't look for evidence showing you otherwise. Instead, start looking for and gathering evidence of your dreams being possible. Artists can make a sh*t ton of money! Engrave that in your mind instead. Choose to believe that your dreams are possible!

Create a mental image in your imagination of your goal achieved, of you being who you want to be: your most divine self! Hold that vision and feel the feeling of being in that moment, as often as you can throughout the day.

Stay true to who you are inside; stay true to your soul's calling! You will always feel inspired when you know your purpose and are striving towards it every single day!

Doesn't it feel good to know your purpose in life? Now we can talk about being in harmony with your purpose and goals!

Harmony

Be in harmony with what you want to create by being on that vibration and frequency. Did you know you are operating on a frequency of vibration? We all are. Everything is in constant vibration! Everything is energy, including you!

You know how when you walk into a room and the energy level makes you feel drained? The people in that room are probably operating at a lower frequency that isn't in harmony with yours. Believe it or not, one negative person can bring down a whole room if everyone in the room allows them to do so by choosing to absorb that person's energy, or if they just automatically/unconsciously let in the energy without realizing it. If you're around someone who has good/high/happy vibrations, you will probably feel that right away as well. It feels good and you enjoy being around them; you want to be around them! You can also choose to absorb this energy, and this is the kind you will want to absorb.

Yes, it is a choice whether we choose to let in people's energy or not. Most of us are used to letting in energy without even being aware that we're allowing it to happen, so it can be challenging to learn how to keep your energy field safe from negative energy.

I know you are probably wondering how to do this. You can keep your energy safe by limiting your transactions with negative people and by deciding that a negative person's energy is not part of your consciousness. It's not your truth, not who you are. You can reject it and decide to stay in your own high vibration. Think, "It's not mine, and I'm choosing to stay in my own beautiful energy!" Staying in a high vibration will actually help to change the energy of the room around you as well. You can actually potentially raise the person's vibration by staying in a high vibration. You are the one who decides who you want to be. If you want to be purely divine with positive energy, no one can stop you from being in that vibration; it's truly a choice. The only one who can stop you is you, so get out of your own way!

Another way to not take on energy is to not give it meaning. If you're focused so hard on trying not to take it in, you are more likely to take it in. Instead, remind yourself of your own beautiful energy and stay in it always! Something important to know is that when you put meaning to something, that's when it usually engraves in your brain. What do I mean by this? Well, when you react to something with an intense emotion (excited, scared, happy, sad), you have placed/given meaning to that thing or situation! I realized that was happening to me when I would hear something negative that I didn't want to have in my brain. Instead of just staying neutral and letting it drift away, I would think about how much I thought it was negative and didn't like it. Well, giving it that meaning made an impression in my mind and made it actually sink into my subconscious mind and stick with me. The easy way is to just let it drift past you like it doesn't mean a thing; it's just neutral. Rather than getting instantly upset about a situation, look at it from a neutral perspective. A neutral perspective will generally help you work through situations easier and will help you stay in harmony with your divine self.

Always be grateful! Being grateful will allow you to feel internally happy, and you will likely operate on a high frequency of vibration. Always strive to stay in that vibration as much as you possibly can!

Be in the vibration of what it is that you want to create. When you are in harmony with what you want to create, with a lot of positive feeling, ways and ideas to express what you want to create will suddenly appear to you in ways you would have never expected. Whether it is in ways/ideas in your mind, or ways in your outer world, the ideas will show. Watch for the signs and signals from the Universe, from God.

"This world is but a canvas to our imagination." This is a quote by American author, Henry David Thoreau. You can truly

create anything you desire with your imagination when you are in divine harmony with it. You are the living embodiment of the sum total of your thoughts! Be one with what it is that you want in life. Embrace it! Become it! Become the person that has already done what you want to do before you even do it! Write down a list of the qualities that you would possess when your goal is achieved. Step into your imagination and imagine what you would be like and how you would feel. That's how you get in harmony, being in the feeling of already having achieved what you want to achieve. Know in your mind it's a done deal, and then success is inevitable. Manifestation is happening!

Now that you are in harmony with what it is that you want, it's time to utilize your imagination to its fullest potential.

Effectively Utilize to the Fullest

It's time to utilize your imagination to the fullest. No more putting your imagination to the side; it's time to bring this beautiful divine faculty to the forefront and elevate your life!

"Logic will get you from A to B. Imagination will take you everywhere." This is a quote by Albert Einstein, and it is so incredibly true! Allow your imagination to wander; that's when you are likely to come up with a new concept or idea. Logic can actually be quite limiting in a sense, but when you utilize your imagination, your world can expand and grow exponentially.

For bonuses go to ...

Your imagination is your most powerful tool, and that's exactly what it is: a tool! We all have it and can all use it to create so much beauty if we choose to do so. Now put it into action!

Sit down, take a few deep breaths, and think. A lot of times, we think that we are thinking, but most of us aren't actually thinking. We allow our outside circumstances and the people around us to think for us, without even realizing it. Get in the habit of asking yourself, "Are those my thoughts or someone else's?" Push their thoughts aside and think for yourself!

Think of all the possibilities in front of you. Think from the point of view of the possibilities being absolutely endless and go from there. Step into your imagination and allow yourself to dream. Create your goal of where you are heading.

Think about what you would love—what you would love to have, love to do, love to be—with no limitations! It can actually be challenging to do this at first because you might start to have doubts and think, "Well, I don't have the money for that," or, "I can't do that; that's not possible." Push through the limiting beliefs and dream big anyway! If anything in the world was possible, what would you be doing and creating? Build from there!

Think about what you would love to create. Your imagination is full of endless possibilities. Allow it to work its magic! Make the decision to let it flow to create the best piece of artwork you possibly can. Give yourself permission to fully utilize your imagination and have fun with it. You can literally create anything you want!

For your art, you can really utilize your imagination by thinking of a concept or object you love. Write it down on a piece of paper. Now think about everything else that comes to mind when you think about that concept or idea. It can be other objects, colours, basically anything. Allow yourself to form a mental image in your mind of all those things related to the concept or object. Play around with it. See if you can arrange those images in your mind to come up with a cohesive way to display your thoughts on a canvas. You will likely create something so amazing and uniquely you! Once you have the finished picture in your mind, do a sketch on a piece of paper so that you don't forget. Be sure to write down details like the colours and shapes you saw. Voila! You utilized your imagination in an expressive way!

Now that you know all about your beautiful imagination, how it works, and how to utilize it, it's time to learn about inspiration and, firstly, how to develop the flow of endless possibilities.

CHAPTER 3

Inspiration

"There is no must in art because art is free."
– Russian painter, Wassily Kandinsky

Develop the Belief of Endless Possibilities

I talked a little bit about possibilities in the first chapter; now we are going to flow right into it! I'll start off by saying one of my favourite lines: "The possibilities are endless!" When you are feeling inspired, your imagination can truly create endless possibilities. Allow yourself to wonder and really adventure into the world of possibilities. There's so much potential waiting for you.

It starts with a belief from within. There are so many different ways to see something; choose to see from a positive angle! Make the decision and choose to believe that the world is full of endless possibilities! This will allow you to be open to receiving different ideas in your mind. Believe me, once you begin to let ideas flow into your imagination on a regular basis, your mind will be like a river; the ideas will just keep flowing! One inspired thought will lead to the next.

Never put a damn on the flow. Allow it to just be! Be in a constant state of flowing possibilities by staying open. I find that when I keep an open mind, ideas begin to flow to me, freely and frequently.

For bonuses go to ...

"The air is full of ideas. They are knocking you in the head all the time. You only have to know what you want, then forget it, and go about your business. Suddenly the ideas will come through. It was there all the time," said Henry Ford, American industrialist and founder of the Ford Motor Company. This is just it; when you put the intention of what you want out into the Universe, ideas will begin to come to you, out of what seems to be air. Ideas might just be soaring through the sky, waiting for you to be open to catch and receive them.

Express what you want to create on your canvas, or in your life. If you need help figuring out what it is that you want, I'd recommend going back to Chapter 2 to re-read "Truly Define Your Purpose." By answering the questions there, you will have a good idea of what it is that you want out of life and would love to create.

Believe that anything is possible! There are no limits! Think from an infinite point of view. The only limits are things like the law of gravity. You don't see cats flying because gravity isn't working today. The law of gravity is always exact, so other than things like that, anything is basically possible as long as you choose to hold that belief.

Ideas are already within you; you just need to become aware of them. As you build your consciousness, you will become aware of more and more within you that was truly there all along, waiting for you to allow it to shine!

It is such a beautiful thing to be absorbed in your imagination and dream. Be brave enough to dream big! Be creative and let endless possibilities flow! People are creating new things all the time; and guess where it starts: within their imaginations! You can create new things too; the possibilities are truly endless!

There is an immense number of possibilities and ideas. It's time to discover them! Now that you hold a belief of endless possibilities in your mind, here are some ideas to help you truly feel inspired.

Ideas to Feel Inspired

Inspiration is EVERYWHERE—like absolutely everywhere! There are so many ideas and ways to feel inspired. Inspiration can be found in nature, in books, in colours, and in absolutely anything you see or do. What does inspiration feel like, though? It's kind of like that "Aha" moment, where an idea strikes you and you feel that "whoa" feeling inside, and you run to find a piece of paper to write down your idea as fast as possible. That's an inspired thought for sure! Another moment of inspiration could be when you're out for a walk and you see something really cool that just makes you feel so warm and fuzzy inside; so you take out your phone to snap a quick photo to hold onto that inspired moment.

It's really beautiful because inspiration can literally strike you at the most interesting moments. For me, it's the moments when

I feel the most calm, happy, relaxed, at ease, and grateful. Those moments are often when I take a warm bath at night, take a walk in nature, clean (I thoroughly enjoy cleaning, as odd as that may sound), and when I cook/bake. These are all things I really enjoy doing aside from my art creations, and they truly help me feel so inspired to create.

Spending time in nature is such a great way to feel inspired! Albert Einstein once said, *"Look deep into nature, and then you will understand everything better."* Nature is so incredibly freeing, happy, and full of colour and life, and inspiration, of course! I highly recommend that you just go out in nature and just be; be you, and be one with nature!

Do something you love, something you thoroughly enjoy doing. By doing something you love (whether it be skateboarding, painting, running, baking, swimming, etc.), you will likely be in a very happy vibration, and this can often help bring out inspiration from within you. Always remember as well that the ideas are already within you; it's just about becoming aware of them!

An interesting way to feel inspired is by looking at your own art. Repurpose your own ideas. Take a look at art you have created. Just a little piece of one of your creations may strike you at that moment to create another entire piece of art based off of one detail from your creation! This has happened to me several times. I've seen the paintings a million times, but one day I'll walk past and certain colours will capture my attention and inspire me to do an entirely new painting based on those colours, or things like the shape of a tree, the flow of wings, swirls, etc. Always be open to inspiration because you never know when it will hit you.

If you're "stuck" on a creation and can't figure out what to do next, just wait; simply just wait and don't try to force it! Know that you will one day find the inspiration of what you would like to do with your creation. Sometimes it takes me a full year of walking past the same painting every single day before the inspiration finally strikes me to finish it. It's well worth the wait because the inspiration that strikes me, and the ideas that have come out of it, are absolutely incredible. Be patient and know that inspiration will come to you.

See everything as potential inspiration. Always look for inspiration in your day-to-day life. When you are focusing on it, you will begin to see it everywhere. The inspiration has always been there; it's up to you to choose to see it!

When you're doing something to feel inspired, always remember to be really present in the moment. Next, you will see why being present and truly valuing moments is so important.

Value the Moments and Be Present

Being really present in the moment and valuing those moments is so important to feel inspired, and to just live a

For bonuses go to ...

fulfilling and happy life in general. We just talked about finding inspiration in nature and other places. Well, in order to see the inspiration in somewhere like nature, you must be really present in the moment! So, basically, when you're not living in your imagination like we talked a lot about in the last chapter, you'll want to be really present and value the moments you have in this time. Moments can be anything, like spending time with family members or a loved one, baking, travelling, dancing, eating, hiking, gardening, etc. Anything you do is basically considered a moment in time.

An example of being present in the moment is when you're out in nature. Really focus on what you see around you. Is there any wildlife, water, trees, mushrooms, birch bark, cool rocks, etc.? Now, what do you smell? Do you smell flowers, trees, the freshness of running water? What about sounds? What do you hear? Birds singing, leaves dancing, complete calmness, crickets, waves? Really take in those moments and enjoy them for what they bring. You can find so much inspiration and peace by just really being present and enjoying what's around you.

Your 5 senses have the chance to experience so many feelings when you are present in the moment, and you never know what they will pick up when you're truly present. You may notice something you wouldn't have noticed if you weren't really present. It's amazing how much beauty you will see when you pay attention to nature.

I know some of this may seem like common sense to just know and do; but truthfully, we often forget to live in the moment and, instead, we get so lost and caught up in our minds and in our daily routines that we forget to slow down and focus on what's right in front of us. We forget to enjoy the present moment. Rather than worrying about life and being on a constant go and rushing it away, focus on what's right in front of you, right at this very moment, and really value and enjoy the moment you are having. Be in a place of just being. It's amazing how calm and content you will feel!

What do you have right now? Be truly grateful for all you are able to do in life, and be grateful for all that life brings! This will truly put you into such a beautiful, happy, emotional state of being.

I know that when I am painting, the experience makes me feel so inspired when I just let the paint brush flow and I really feel each stroke of the brush—not thinking of anything else, but just being; allowing myself to be in a calm state at that very moment and enjoying the experience of painting to the fullest!

Find the good in all you do. There is good in every moment! Even if you don't see it at first, it will show itself later on. I am a firm believer in everything happening for a reason. Life brings lessons and blessings. Enjoy whichever one each moment brings; after all, you are the creator of your life, and you choose what you create. If you're not happy, choose to make a change and create a different moment.

Always know where you are going and live in the moment. Now you will be able to allow your imagination to flow effortlessly and be in a state of flow. You will feel so inspired! Let's talk about that now.

In a State of Flow

When you're constantly on the go, just living your day-to-day routine (almost like a robot on autopilot), it may not be as easy to come up with great ideas; they may become slightly blocked in a sense. If you want to be in a state of flow, choose to slow down sometimes, and make the time to do something you love and something that makes your soul happy. Focus solely on that, and it will be a lot easier to be in a creative state of flow by doing so.

Make the decision to allow your mind to drift into a creative state. When your imagination is flowing, never neglect it or try to turn off the faucet! Allow ideas to flow freely as they will. You want your imagination to stay in a flow so that ideas will come easily and effortlessly. Never use force either. Sometimes you've got to give your mind the time to create; be patient! Remember to imagine all the potential possibilities out there that are within your reach; open your eyes to them! Your imagination will generate beautiful ideas and create such a beautifully inspired state of flow within you.

Choose to stay in an inspired state of flow as much as possible. The more you stay in the flow, the more natural it will become, and the more it will be a part of your everyday life! Inspiration and new ideas will appear often when you are in a state of flow, and that will help you exponentially in your life, and as an artist.

Thomas A. Edison quoted, *"To have a great idea, have a lot of them."* The way I perceive this quote is that truly, if you keep coming up with ideas, you're sure to have a new and great one! Even if it's not the first, keep thinking; keep utilizing your imagination while you're in a state of flow. Also, when you start thinking of ideas often, they will start to come more frequently as well. I've found this with myself, that when I allow my mind to be in a creative state and create beautiful ideas for my art, the more often I do it, the more my mind automatically wants to do it.

Open the floodgates of your imagination! Your imagination can truly do wonders to think of beautiful creations if you let yourself wonder. "Wait, you're talking about the imagination again?" Yes! Imagination and inspiration go hand in hand. Your imagination will literally just flow when you are feeling inspired, and you will feel inspired by being in a beautiful state of flow. Sounds odd, I know, but it's very true!

When you are in a state of flow, the way will seem effortless... the "effortless way." The effortless way is when you're moving in the right direction with so much ease and flow.

It's finding the path of least resistance! Think of creating something. This is when your mind will toss around a lot of possibilities with ease. Formulate the ideas together to create a painting!

Always keep a pen/pencil and paper close by; when you are in a state of flow, the best ideas will show themselves. When these ideas arrive, that's when it's time to take inspired and aligned actions. We will look into that in the next chapter, but before that, now that you are in a state of flow, you can begin to think in an extraordinary way. Think outside the box! We will talk about this next.

Naturally Think Outside the Box

Now that you're in a state of flow and feeling so inspired, you can think outside the box! Think of the extraordinary, where anything is possible and anything goes. The only limitation, like I mentioned before, is something like the law of gravity. We know it's exact every single time. I know there are a lot of social standards of what art is "supposed" to look like, and we tend to have these preconceived ideas of what art truly is, because of that. Well, it's time to shove those limiting thoughts aside; they aren't serving you in any way whatsoever! It's time to truly think! This is where your creative imagination comes into play; so play around with it a bit and have some fun!

Here's an example of thinking outside the box for creating: In high school art class, one of my best friends literally created a dinosaur out of old scratch tickets (like a huge dinosaur) for an art project. Like, who would have thought to do something like that! That's thinking on an extraordinary level for sure. I chose to make an edible rainbow out of desserts for one of my art projects. I used a peanut butter crispy treat for the base of the rainbow, and I painted it with different coloured icing. Then, I melted marshmallows and stuck those around the base for clouds. I put white icing across the marshmallows to make it look magical and refined, and then used icing to make the blue sky across the bottom. Art is so open! I know people have created art out of Rubik's cubes, sand, and just really different materials that we may not generally think of right away, to create with. Maybe think about a type of new material or item you can use to paint with instead of a paint brush, or even something to use instead of paint. The possibilities are truly endless!

In life, if you keep thinking the same thoughts every single day, you're likely to keep having the same results. Choose to think outside the box, and don't be afraid to be unconventional! Think about someone like Thomas Edison, who invented the incandescent light bulb. That's some extremely extraordinary thinking on his behalf; a totally new idea that has absolutely changed the world! Guess what? We all have the power to create anything we want! You can truly change the world with your own thoughts and ideas. Believe in yourself; if you don't believe in yourself, believe that I believe in you!

For bonuses go to ...

Want to know something amazing? Every new idea triggers additional ideas. You will feel so inspired when you have idea after idea. The possibilities are endless!

Remember back in "Truly Define Your Purpose," where we talked about thinking in a way of defining your purpose? Revisit that chapter bullet and see what you answered for the questions in that section. I challenge you to think outside the box and stretch those goals and purpose even further, and think of the extraordinary. If your goal doesn't scare you, it's not big enough! Make it a goal that scares and excites you at the same time. Make it a goal that you don't know how you will achieve it, but you want to achieve it, and you know you will achieve it somehow: it becomes a burning desire! Then you'll know it's a good goal/purpose if you want to live an extraordinary life.

Now that you are inspired from thinking outside the box, it's time to elevate yourself by trying something new. Let's jump right into this!

Elevate by Trying Something New

You may be nervous or afraid to try something new because you have a fear of failure. When you become aware of being fearful, you can overcome it! The reality is, we all have to start somewhere, and we are all ongoing learners in this Universe!

Everything starts with trying, so just simply try—what do you have to lose? Yes, I realize there is always a risk in trying something new, but if you don't try, you risk staying in the same place, and your life will remain the same. I challenge you to risk trying something new, something different! The thing is, either way, there is a risk involved in everything, so you will be taking a risk regardless. Choose your risk wisely; I encourage you to bet on yourself for once! *"You are not the risk, you are the investment,"* as said by Jenna Kutcher, online marketing expert and *New York Times* bestselling author. You can gain so much growth from simply just trying.

"Be brave enough to be bad at something new," says Jon Acuff, leadership speaker and *New York Times* bestselling author. Be brave enough to simply try. Everything is truly worth a shot! It is said that every success starts with the decision to try. Even if things don't work out the first time quite how you wanted them to, it's just the beginning; it's part of your learning process and growth! You become stronger and stronger every time you choose to be brave!

Trying something new can help you define what you like to do and what you don't like to do. This is true for both your canvas and your life.

For your creativity, surrender to the process by just trying something new and experimenting. You may find a love for a certain way of creating (different techniques, different colour mixings, and different styles). Just have fun with it! As Russian painter Wassily Kandinsky once said, *"There is no must in art because art is free."* Be free for once and try something new!

For bonuses go to ...

Anything can go; there are so many possibilities. You can create on several different surfaces, such as birch bark, canvas, rocks, wood, etc. As for creative materials, you will learn what tools you love to use, what mediums you enjoy working with, the colours and tones you enjoy, and the shapes, effects, etc., that you love.

As an artist, I have tried several different mediums, such as acrylic paint, oil paint, watercolour paint, sketching pencils and charcoal, ink with an ink pen, etc. By trying these different mediums, I found out what I loved and what I didn't love! I didn't enjoy using oil paints because they take an incredibly long time to dry, and I kept smudging the artwork. The watercolours also took too long to dry for me and are too muted for my love of colour. That's how I landed on loving acrylic paint, and that's why I have been painting with acrylics for over 14 years. Acrylic paint dries really fast, which is super convenient to work with, and the colours are incredibly vivid—after all, my mission in life is to empower people to embody colourful and easy lives so that they will live with joy and inspiration. So, there you go, very fitting indeed, and I'm so glad that I experienced different ways of creating to find out what I loved most!

The point is, when you go through the process of these new experiences, trust the process. You will gain so much inspiration for trying something new and you will really figure out what you love.

In life, trying something new will help you define what you love to do in life and what you would love to experience. You may try baking and find out that you absolutely enjoy it wholeheartedly. You may try painting portraits and find a love for that. The possibilities are endless! Trying something new is always so exciting! You will be incredibly inspired from having these different experiences of trying something new. You will only regret what you didn't try, and with trying new things, when you know, you'll know! Your heart will let you know when something feels right for you. You'll have that intuitive feeling in your gut. What is intuition anyway? You're about to find out!

I have created free bonuses to go along with this incredible book. Find them at www.EmpoweredCreatorBook.com.

CHAPTER 4

Intuition

"The best and most beautiful things in the world cannot be seen or even touched; they must be felt with the heart."
– Helen Keller

Awaken Your Intuition

Intuition? What is it? Just like your imagination, your intuition is one of your higher faculties of thinking. It separates you from the rest of the animal kingdom. If you are aware of these faculties and utilize them in beautiful ways, you can exponentially change your life for the better!

Intuition is the ability to understand something instantly without the need for reasoning. In my opinion, you just know! It's your awareness of that gut feeling within you that's telling you to do something or to not do something. It's basically an instinctive feeling instead of conscious reasoning. It's when you follow your heart and let God work through you.

If you choose to spend time reasoning, you will likely go back and forth in your head about what you should do. It's like the analogy of the little angel and devil sitting on each of your shoulders, trying to tell you what to do and bouncing your mind back and forth on what the right decision is, and reasoning against each other. This is ambivalence and basically leads to indecision, which can be paralyzing. Knowing what you want will set your mind at ease, so instead of reasoning, simply do what feels right inside! It's literally that simple! If it doesn't feel good when you're doing it, you should probably stop and make a different choice and look at a different path, as you are likely not on the right one. Intuition will always tell you if you're on the right path by the feeling you have inside you. Your inner self knows what's best! If what you're currently doing in life doesn't light up your heart and set your soul on fire, it is probably not what you truly want to do and are meant to be doing. You just need to make the decision to be who you truly want to be. As said often by the late Bob Proctor, *"The only prerequisite of a decision is whether you want it or not."*

I know it can be easy to get caught in a psychological cycle of needing to know every detail of why you should do something, why you shouldn't do something, and the how of achieving something. We sometimes get carried away and over-think situations. The best advice I've ever gotten from my brother is, "Don't over-think it!" He gave that advice to me about a driving situation, but I tend to think about it often and utilize it in several different situations in my life.

A prime example of when I personally used my intuition was when I joined a webinar about branding. I instantly knew within me that the program following it was my next step. The feeling was so strong and I didn't fully understand why it was my next step, but I 100% knew inside my heart and soul that it just felt right and was the right step for me to take in that moment. This is why sometimes it's better to push aside the "why" and just trust your intuition because it is guiding you to where you're meant to be! It turns out that the branding program wasn't just a branding process; it was an entire self-discovery journey for me. I discovered so much about myself. The Branding Foundations Program was actually where I created the 4 I's, as I mentioned in the first chapter. This book probably wouldn't be what it is today if it wasn't for me choosing to listen to my intuition, my gut feeling, and take that program. I could have chosen to not invest in myself and look the other way, but instead, I listened! Every bit of my soul was telling me to take the program, and I listened without a shadow of a doubt. I just simply knew, made the decision, and took action, and I am so glad I did!

Next time you're about to make a decision or do something, really pay attention to how you're feeling in that instance. Are you sad, upset, nauseous, or queasy when just thinking about a certain path? Yup, don't go down it! On the other hand, though, if you're feeling happy, content, grateful, pulled towards something (there's no hesitation), and have that gut feeling telling you it's the right thing to do, you're likely meant to go down that path!

Now that you know what intuition is, it's important to know why you should always listen and follow your heart.

For bonuses go to ...

Resonate and Follow Your Heart

It's incredibly important to listen to your heart. Why, you may ask? The good that you desire will come from doing so! You will intuitively attract everything and everyone you need in your life to take the next step to your success.

Do what resonates with you! Always listen to your heart and soul; they always know what's best. Let ideas actually come from your heart and not from external circumstances. If you're always worrying about what other people will think, you are probably making decisions based on their opinions instead of your own. Push everyone else's opinions aside and go within—follow your heart! Be consciously aware of your intuition because it is your inner guide and will lead you on the path of least resistance. Allow it to show you the effortless way! When you listen to your intuition, it will guide you to what you truly want inside. Allow yourself to be guided, even if it's not what you had originally thought or planned. Sometimes you just have to go with the flow of what's happening at the moment and listen to your heart.

Not everything has to have a reason beforehand. When something feels right within your heart, do that! I know you may like to analyze things and reason ahead of time before making decisions, but it's time to put your analytical mind aside for once. For the decisions you make in life, your heart will know what you truly want, if you choose to listen to it. Plus, it is known that successful people make decisions quickly and change them slowly if and when they do this.

"The best and most beautiful things in the world cannot be seen or even touched; they must be felt with the heart" is a quote by Helen Keller. That's just it; the feeling you get from doing what you love will be so incredible when you choose what your heart truly desires—not what anyone else wants for you, but what you want for you!

Just like we talked about before, your intuition is that gut feeling within, telling you when something feels good or when something feels off and is not right. Some people call it their intuitive heart and believe that it is far more important than their mind when it comes to decision making. I know personally that I sometimes have intuitive hits that just tell me to do something at that very moment. Usually, it's something completely out of my comfort zone, and my intuition gives me that push to know that it's the right decision or action to take at that moment. I may not know why at the time, but I usually find out the purpose of the intuitive hit, afterwards, and I am always glad that I listened!

Some people believe that the heart basically has its own brain within it. It kind of makes sense, doesn't it? Signals that come from the heart, those gut feelings, are instinctively speaking to you to help you make the best decision possible.

All in all, I wholeheartedly believe that when you choose to listen to your heart and do what resonates with your soul, you'll always be headed in the right direction on your journey. Even if a decision may seem scary at the time, it will make sense soon enough.

For bonuses go to ...

Allow your heart and your intuition to truly guide you. You will attract so many beautiful ideas! *"The value of an idea is in the using of it,"* as stated by Thomas Edison. Next, you will learn about taking inspired and aligned actions with your ideas.

Take Inspired and Aligned Actions

Aligned action is key when it comes to moving towards your goals and creations! You can have all the thoughts and ideas in the world, but until you take action on them, they will usually stay as a thought in your mind. As soon as you begin to take aligned action, you can turn your ideas into a reality. It was said by Spanish painter, Pablo Picasso, *"Action is the foundational key to all success."* It is true; success will come to you from taking the right actions! I've learned very much that in order to become successful, you need to stop procrastinating and do what you know you're meant to do. Success is generally on the other side of fear. I believe I heard that through speaker Sandy Gallagher. Go against the fear and know that one step leads to the next! You don't need to see the whole ladder or staircase, just keep climbing and you will continue to be shown the next step. In other words, you don't need to know the "how" of how you will reach a goal. Just take aligned actions! Aligned actions are small steps at a time towards your goal in mind. It's what you already know can be done to move towards it, and once you take action on that, it will lead you to your next actionable step to take. One small step at a time will lead you to big results!

Inspired action is when you feel pulled towards something to take action on it, and you listen to that feeling and take the action. It's your intuition talking to you; it's God working through you, guiding you to take the next right step on your journey. When you take inspired action, you will be so motivated and in such a beautiful vibration that you will create the most amazing things in your life, and in your artistic world as well. I highly recommend taking action when you have an inspired thought, a thought from God. You won't regret taking actions, but you will regret not taking the actions you know you are meant to take. Don't hesitate! Just do it; you've got this!

Visualize the outcome of what you want your creation to look like, but be willing to be flexible. Things may change as you go. Along the way, an inspired thought may hit, and intuition might pull you to take you on a different path/direction than you had originally imagined. Let it happen! Allow things to unfold as they are supposed to! You'll be surprised at the creation you end up with. I find that when I'm flexible about the outcome, so much more happens when I take action, and the artwork becomes way more beautiful and unique than it would have been, if I had strictly followed what I visualized the artwork to look like at the beginning. Basically, what you need to do is know the outcome of what you want your creation to look like, but detach yourself from the outcome. This way, you won't have your mind set so strong on what the art should look like in the end, and you'll stay more open to change. Inspired ideas may form along the way.

For bonuses go to ...

Do something you love and thoroughly enjoy doing! While doing so, you will likely feel happy, relaxed, calm, and fulfilled. Feeling this way will likely bring you inspired thoughts. When you're feeling this way, put the intention in the air that you would like to create a piece of art. Start thinking of colours, shapes, etc., that just make sense to you at that very moment. Start visualizing a creation in your mind. As soon as you have a creation in mind, sketch it out. Take action to turn this creation into a reality. Grab a paintbrush, pencil, fountain pen and ink, whatever it is you choose to create with, and go at it! If not, at least grab a pen and notebook to sketch out what it is that you want to create, to remember your amazing ideas and to take action at another time when you are feeling inspired again.

Now that you know the importance of taking inspired, aligned actions, let's push past any perfectionism you are holding onto!

Initiate Letting Go of Perfection

First of all, what is perfectionism? Well, in my eyes, it is having to make things "perfect" and not wanting to settle for anything less than the imagined picture or idea of "perfection" that you hold. It's your perception of what you consider to be absolutely flawless, with no mistakes, and completely and utterly perfect.

Having your focus stuck only on the idea of perfection can really limit what you can create in your art world and in your life!

I mean, I guess perfectionism can be a blessing in some cases, like if you're creating a very precise wedding cake for someone. In the end, though, nothing is truly perfect anyway. Well, then again, God sees us all as perfection. Otherwise, though, nothing is truly perfect, so focus on taking imperfect actions to maximize your full potential of what you can achieve. Even if it's not "perfect" and up to "your standards," choose to see what you have done through the lens of God- perfection.

Perfectionism can be a weakness in a way. I used to use that example in interviews for jobs. When the interviewers asked me what a bad quality about myself was, I always said that I'm a perfectionist. When they asked how that could be a bad thing, I always mentioned that I sometimes took longer to do things because I wanted it to be so perfect and refined. The reality of perfection is that trying to be perfect can be exhausting, limiting, unenjoyable, and as I mentioned before, very time-consuming! Also, by telling myself that I'm a perfectionist, I am only encouraging and solidifying that behavior even more within myself if I choose to see myself in such a way.

For some reason, we tend to get caught up in social standards and the way others think our art should be. We may fear judgement of others and/or have a fear of failure or fear of success. It's interesting how we do this; we basically self-sabotage what we're truly capable of creating, by having these fears. Fear makes us play it safe with our art and not truly express what we're meant to express from within. Initiate letting go of your idea of perfection and society's idea of "perfect." Push past and just be open to change, and let your creative mind flow! Let go and express who you truly are: your truth! You are capable of bringing so much love, joy, happiness, and positive expression to the world. It's time to embrace that fact!

So, all in all, how can you deal with perfectionism? Start by reminding yourself of your truth! Always remember that the self-image you have when you're in a perfectionist state, is not the self-image of who you are when you achieve all of your goals: your truth, your divine self! Let go of seeing yourself as a perfectionist and focus on seeing yourself in a different way! See yourself as someone who is growing every day! Focus on being 1% better and moving 1% closer to your goal by taking imperfect action every single day.

Let go of what's not serving you, like the thought of trying to make something "perfect," and of whatever concept and belief that you have in your head of what you feel "perfect" is. Let go and let loose, go with the flow, trust yourself, and have fun with it!

Whenever perfectionism decides to kick back in, give yourself grace when it happens. It's okay; just try to worry less about the perfect standard in your mind, and give yourself permission to not be perfect. I know you may have high expectations for yourself, but it's okay not to be perfect. What is important though is to keep moving forward! Now that you can tackle most of your perfectionism, it's time to tackle the last part of perfectionism: knowing when a piece of artwork or creation is complete.

Stop and Know When It's Complete

It can be challenging to know when something is complete, especially when you see yourself as a perfectionist! Luckily, we just tackled perfectionism, but this is a big part of it too. I didn't even think of this aspect of perfectionism until I was talking with some of my perfectionist friends, and I realized how important this aspect is to talk about. How do you know when to stop painting? How do you know when it's complete? It's time to use your intuition and know from within!

To know when a creation is complete, it can be as simple as the feeling. It's that gut feeling inside; it's your intuition telling you that your creation is beautiful exactly how it is, and to not change anything.

For me, personally, I take lots of breaks when I'm making an art creation, and I step back and just look at it often. I literally step away and stare at my creation to see how it makes me feel inside, especially when I feel that it is getting close to being complete. When I look at my creation, if it feels good and makes me feel whole and happy inside, then it is likely complete. If your heart is telling you to stop and leave it as it is, it's for a reason, and I recommend listening! If it feels good but doesn't feel quite right yet, then that means that something is likely missing. It just doesn't feel quite whole, and your gut keeps telling you that it's not done yet. Take the time to figure out what's missing. Even if you set it aside for a whole year until you have the inspiration of what's missing on it, to finish it, do that. Do what you need to do! Take the time to find the inspiration; it is well worth it in the end. Your intuition will always guide you in the right direction, so always trust it!

I know you may keep feeling like it's not enough and that it has to be perfect, but that's where fear of failure, success, and judgement are taking a toll on your mind! If you feel someone is judging you and your art, it's generally a reflection of how you see and feel about yourself, mirroring back at you. For example, if you feel that you're unworthy, people will likely see you as unworthy. If you're afraid of judgement, you will likely always feel judged. Feeling judged is a choice. Only you can decide to feel judged by what someone says to you. Choose to be neutral and not give their words or actions any meaning! Also, the truth is that people's judgements are a reflection of their own consciousness and self-image. Try not to take it personally; they may be afraid to do what they want to in life and are judging you because they are secretly jealous of your bravery. Who cares how others perceive you! At the end of the day, the only opinion of you that matters is your own, a.k.a. your self-image (how you perceive yourself). See yourself as the divine artist you truly are! You know your truth, so brush off the judgements, pick yourself up, and keep shining your beautiful and unique light in the world! The world needs your genuineness and creativity! See your worth and people will begin to see your worth as well.

Another way to tell when a creation is done, is when you've accomplished the motive you have for your creation. This is when you've captured exactly what you wanted to capture, within your creation, like a concept or idea. You know it's done and feel it within your heart and soul. For example, if you are to create something to spread awareness about pollution in the ocean, you'll want it to display that message within your creation. If you look at your creation and it screams that message, without a shadow of a doubt, anyone who looks at your creation will see the message you are portraying, then you've done what you were striving to do. Let the creation be; it is done and amazing!

Knowing when a creation is complete is huge. Knowing when to stop is much better than sitting there for hours adding more and more to your creation to try and make it "perfect." That just becomes overwhelming, and there is a saying, "Sometimes less is more." This holds to be true in some situations, so keep this in mind for certain creations. Sometimes the simplest ideas create the biggest impact, especially when you allow your intuition to guide you. When you listen to your intuition and follow your heart, you may end up going against the grain in some cases. What's the grain? Let's jump into that next!

For bonuses go to ...

To Go Against the Grain

Sometimes utilizing your intuition and listening to your heart will mean that you will go against the grain. Going against the grain in life is basically when you differ from the crowd; you do something that may seem unconventional and unorthodox. Who's the crowd? The crowd is the general population. Going against the grain means that you choose to be different from what the social norm is, and different from what's considered to be socially acceptable and normal.

Sometimes we tend to become complacent to how society thinks we should be. We end up living our day-to-day lives doing what is considered normal. For example, after high school, we're told to go to college or university to get an education so that we can get jobs in a certain field. Who the heck decided that we have to do that! Society makes it sound like that is our only option to take. Don't get me wrong; I went to college straight after high school, when I was only 17 years old, and it was a great life experience! The thing is, though, I just picked a course that was the "best option" at the time, because I truly didn't know what I wanted to do with my life at that point. I thought I had to pick something because I was supposed to go to college like everyone else; I picked something that seemed fitting to make a potential career out of, which would make me a certain amount of money each year.

This is where you need to let go and let your intuition guide you, not society! Maybe college/university is for you if you're taking a program that involves your passion, but maybe it's not for you. In your heart, how do you truly want to spend your life? Even if you don't know how doing what you love could possibly make you a living, explore your options regardless. Anything is possible! What is it that you want to create in your life and on your canvas?

Unconventionality means "original." For example, original artwork comes from thinking of your own ideas, thinking outside of the box, and potentially going against the grain as well. The concept of going against the grain can seem scary! You may catch yourself thinking things like, "What will others think?" "Will they love this new thing that I am doing or think I'm weird and want nothing to do with me?" Whoa, whoa, whoa; hold up a minute! If you have ever had thoughts like that, it's time to choose to let them go! Be open to a new possible truth. The truth is, going against the grain is actually super fun! It's so fun to be your own person and not be afraid of judgement. It's very freeing to just be you, and to stop living the way everyone expects you to live and, instead, live the way YOU truly want to live! It takes courage and bravery to do this. Try taking the first step of bravery and courage today! Maybe it's something you've thought about trying but have been too scared to actually attempt, so you end up procrastinating and avoiding it. JUMP into it with your whole heart and soul! Like I mentioned before, if people have an opinion about what you're doing, it's generally just a reflection of their own self-image. Maybe they're jealous because they're too scared to do what they truly want to do in their life. In this case, just keep doing what you're doing and remember that people's opinions of you are none of your business!

Personally, I want to be different. If I follow the crowd, I will be just like everyone else around me. How boring would it be if we all did the same things? A world full of everything and everyone the same—yikes! Choose to shine your uniqueness to the world!

Make, create, and bring something new to the world—something you! Your heart may lead you in a certain direction that's different from a standard way of living, and that's okay. Be brave enough to follow your intuition and do what feels right in your heart. Even if it feels unconventional and unorthodox, do it anyway!

Now that you're more comfortable with the thought of being different and going against the grain, you can ignite your authenticity. Let's do this!

CHAPTER 5

Ignite

"You know more than you know you know!"
– Price Pritchett, Ph.D.

Wonderfully Authentic

Being authentic is when you are being completely genuine to who you are. It's about being confident enough to share who you are with others, without holding back. It's about being true to yourself regardless of what anyone else is doing, and regardless of what anyone else says. Being wonderfully authentic starts with knowing who you are!

So, who are you right now? Who is the person you are stepping into? The person that has already done what you want to do, before you even do it? What is your truth? These can feel like big questions, but I would love for you to truly think about it! Sit down with a pen and paper and answer them the best you can. Start by figuring out who you are in this moment. List the qualities you have at this moment. Once you figure out who you are, figure out who you want to be. What qualities does that person have? I know you answered this question in Chapter 2's section, "Harmony," but I would love for you to look at your answers again and expand on them. It's time to step into that person and embody your new identity! Embody the person you want to become before becoming him/her! This will close the gap faster, and you will become who you're truly meant to be, in a quantum leap.

Always be true to yourself; be true to who you are! Be brave enough to be you and shine your light to the world! I saw on a plaque not too long ago, "To be a star, you must shine your own light." I love this! I bought the little plaque for my niece. No matter how weird or different you may think you are, shine your light anyway. There are people out there who will resonate with you and what you will bring to the world. You would actually be doing a disservice to these people if you don't show who you are and show up for them. They need to hear your story! Someone out there needs to hear or see what you have to say, offer, or show. You have a bigger gift than you may realize, and you can help so many people once you become aware of your gift and become aware of the potential you have to impact several people's lives. You can help so many people by just being authentic and showing them who you truly are. You have so much potential, just waiting to be set free! Be fearless and realize that you have something amazing and so special to bring to the world! It's your time to shine!

For your art and creations, let your authenticity shine! I'm a colourful person who loves inspiration and nature, and that's what absolutely sparkles in my art. Anyone who sees my artwork can tell that about me. It's very apparent in my art. Add your personality and your vibrations to your creations. People will feel who you are by looking at your artwork. I can always tell how a person thinks through the artwork they produce. People stuck in a negative vortex tend to have darker looking creations with a darker meaning. Joyful, positive people tend to have happy, flowy, and bright artwork. What kind of art would you like to produce? Who will you choose to be? If you don't like who you are, you have the power to change and be a better person every single day. The choice is yours, and it starts with a decision!

Separate yourself from others. Sometimes we can get caught in a whirlwind of wanting to be like someone else, and we try to follow someone else's roadmap. Here's the truth, though: Only you can be you, so choose to be you, and that is your truth! I kind of sound like Dr. Seuss by saying that. All in all, be truly authentic always, and let your authenticity shine within your art and creations. I know this can take bravery and courage to do, so let's step into that right now.

Infinite Bravery and Boldness

Even when it feels like there's a metaphorical fire burning around you, be brave anyway! Stand taller than the fire! You are brave and courageous!

One big moment of bravery that I took in the past was when I decided to get a vehicle and actually start driving. Before that, I had just driven a couple of times here and there if I really had to, and mostly just in the small town I'm from. The furthest I had driven at that point was 15 minutes away on the highway. I was just so nervous about anything that had to do with me driving.

For bonuses go to ...

One day, I woke up and literally said, "F*ck this!" Pardon my language, but it literally came to that point where I was absolutely done with being afraid. The desire for independence became stronger than my fear. I took my parents' vehicle and drove 15 minutes one way on the highway to a beach, and I sat there reading my driver's book. Then I drove about 25 minutes the other way to go to a lookout, and then I drove back home.

The next day, I let my parents know that I was going to go to the city with them. They were planning to go to Thunder Bay, 2 hours away from Schreiber! I mentioned that I was going to drive. They were incredibly shocked, and nervous obviously. This would be the first time for me driving in the city. I woke up and drove the 2 hours there (longest I had ever driven all at once on the highway), drove around the city all day, and then drove home in the dark and in the rain! Oh, and while I was there, I picked out my dream vehicle and had it placed on order! That was probably the bravest I've ever felt, and I haven't looked back since. Why did I tell you this story? To inspire you, because sometimes you've just got to say, "F*ck fear," and take action! Literally toss fear out the window and decide that your wants and desires are stronger than fear!

My brother gave me the best advice in the world before that day as well. When I asked him about city driving, he said, "Don't over-think it." It was literally the simplest comment and concept, but it made the biggest impact on my life at the time, and I still think of it all the time for several other situations now. I invite you to think of that the next time you catch yourself in a fearful, over-thinking situation. Stop yourself and silence the over-thinking with that one comment—"don't over-think it"—and just take action!

Think of a time when you felt that you were brave. Hold that feeling in your mind and use it as evidence that you can be brave again and again.

When it comes to creating, creating is limitless! Go above and beyond! Try something new; don't be afraid to do something different than what you're used to seeing be done by others and what society considers to be acceptable to do. Don't be afraid to have fun with your artwork. Be brave to try something different!

Something that a lot of people tend to struggle with is procrastinating. Procrastinating, to me, means that there's resistance and fear hidden within you. You are pushing aside what you should be doing at the time, due to fear, and creating every "valid" excuse in the book for why you haven't done it yet. Stop doing that! Get out of your own way! If you recognize that you should do something, you feel within your heart that you should do it, and you know it will benefit your future, then be brave and just do it! You can literally do anything you put your mind to, regardless of how scary it may seem, and generally, afterwards, you will feel like, "Oh, that was it? That wasn't so bad!" So just do it! Oftentimes, we play things up in our heads to be a lot scarier or harder to do than they actually are. Choose to see things as easy and light. You will only regret what you didn't do. By choosing to push past fear, and to be brave and bold, you will develop confidence to be brave and bold again and again, even more often in the future. You will feel unstoppable! Be sure to make bravery so strong that fear is obsolete and just disintegrates because you're no longer focusing on it. There will only be room for being brave and bold!

It's easier to be brave and bold when you believe in yourself, so now it's time to start believing!

Time to Believe in Yourself

Ignite the artist within you! Spark your imagination, inspiration, and intuition; it all starts from within! You are a true artist, you are creative, and there are so many possibilities for your beautiful imagination to create. It's time to believe in yourself!

Just like we talked about at the very beginning, everything that occurs in your life starts within your imagination. One thing that starts within your imagination is what you imagine to be true about yourself. It's interesting how we feel about ourselves sometimes; our perspectives (self-image) tend to differ from other people's perspectives of us. What you decide to be true about yourself will highly affect how you show up in your everyday life. If you decide that you're not confident, you will show up unconfident. If you decide that you're brave and you're ready to take on the world, that's exactly what you'll do. It all comes down to how you feel about yourself.

If you don't have a good concept of yourself, decide to change your self-image. You can do this by writing down the qualities you have now, from a neutral standpoint so that you're not feeling bad or judged about it. Just be as neutral and as truthful as you can! You've done this for the most part already, and I'm sure your list keeps expanding along the way. Now write down your strengths and weaknesses. Then write down "I am…," with the opposite of what the weaknesses are. This will turn your weaknesses into strengths overtime through autosuggestion! For example, if you want to be braver with your art, tell yourself, "I am brave!" It may feel weird and like you don't believe yourself at first, but keep doing it every single day with as much emotion and conviction as you can, until you truly believe it. YOU are brave!

If it's you that has said negative things to yourself in the past, in your mind, that's called self-talk! Start paying attention to the way you speak to yourself. I realized I would call myself an "idiot" if I accidentally dropped something! I would never say that to someone else, so why was I saying it to myself? That was a big realization for me! Self-talk is highly important because it takes a huge toll on your self-image, how you see yourself, just as though it had been said by someone close to you. Even if you are "joking," your subconscious mind will still take it in as truth. It doesn't know the difference between being serious and joking, so it just takes in all information as truth. If you have said things that put yourself down, or things to hold yourself back, give yourself grace and forgive yourself for doing so. This will allow you to move past them and let them go. Choose to be the best

For bonuses go to ...

version of yourself that you can be, from now on. Be 1% better every day. Speak as kindly to yourself as you would to others!

As I was writing this book, I genuinely thought to myself, "Do I truly know enough about the imagination to write this many pages about it?" Then I remembered a handbook that I had read by Price Pritchett, PH.D., called *You ^{2}*, which said, "You know more than you know you know." I knew this was true and began to write, and everything flowed to me with ease every time I sat down to write! This is true for you too! You have the resources! You may not know you have them until you act, but everything you need is already within you. Truly believe in yourself with your whole heart!

If you still can't believe in yourself, like I've said before, believe that I believe in you! YOU are incredible! Me telling you this won't do much, though; tell it to yourself. Bring in auto-suggestion again, and even if you don't believe it at first, just keep telling yourself every single day, "I believe in myself," until you do believe in yourself, because you will! Doing it in the mirror makes it even stronger and adds more feeling to it. Look at yourself in the mirror, every morning and every night, and say "I am" affirmations of who you want to be. For example, "I am brave, I am bold, I am confident, I am worthy, I am an empowered creator, I am a powerful artist!" It may feel really weird and uncomfortable at first, but it gets easier as you do it more and more, because you truly start to believe it!

Oprah Winfrey said, *"What God intended for you goes far beyond anything you can imagine."* Believe you can achieve anything you set your mind to! Give yourself a shot in life! Choose to believe in yourself wholeheartedly! Everything you need, to be an empowered creator, is already within you! Step into it! Take the jump and be who you are meant to be!

Now that you believe in yourself, you can definitely come up with your own ideas in art, and you will become aware of it right now!

Have Your Own Ideas

Thinking of your own ideas may be a challenge at first. I feel that most of us start out in art by copying other ideas off the internet and using those as a template to create something. That's not an original piece of art because you are not the artist who came up with the idea in the first place. It's more of a learning process in my opinion.

I realized that I used to get so frustrated in high school when my art teacher would tell us to come up with our own ideas, and I would think, "Okay, sure, but how?" I feel like the "how" is always left out!

So how do you have your own ideas? My suggestion is to let your imagination run wild. Be open to infinite possibilities at any given time during the day!

For bonuses go to ...

We talked about an idea similar to this, near the beginning. Start with a piece of paper to come up with an idea. Perhaps think of a concept, idea, or an emotion that you like, and branch off from there. For example, if you choose the emotion "happy," think of things that you associate with the word "happy." When I think of happiness, I think of sunshine, rainbows, butterflies, cupcakes, the colour yellow, etc. Write down all of the ideas you come up with! Now take a look at the ideas you came up with and see what feels good together, and see what resonates with you and what you would love to create with it. Start to sketch out an image of how all your ideas could mesh together cohesively on a canvas. Do a couple of sketches if you want to have a couple of different ideas to play around with. Now, go into this creation with your idea in mind, but remember to detach yourself from the outcome. Allow ideas, and/or your paintbrush (or any artistic tool of choice), to just flow as you keep creating! Who knows, your imagination may come up with something new that you hadn't thought about in the planning stage. Just go with the flow and don't over-think it! Your creation will be incredible!

For me, ideas just flow to me at all times of the day now, especially if I place an intention for them to come. If I'm doing something I thoroughly enjoy doing, like going for a walk, while I'm walking, I will often ask myself, "What could I paint?" Then I continue to be grateful for where I am and be really present in that moment. Oftentimes, I will see something that inspires me, or an idea will shoot right to me. I stop and either take a photo or write down my ideas in my phone until I can get back home to write it on paper. That's another option as well, to do something you enjoy doing very much and ask that question to place the intention of new ideas coming to your mind.

Take your own photos of nature, buildings, boats, etc., and look at those to paint. This is a great way to create your own idea as well. I know some people will print out their photos and draw a grid across them. Then they draw a grid across their canvas or sketchbook to know where to paint everything on it.

As you continue to come up with your own ideas, you will become really good at doing so; your mind will be racing a lot, especially when you are feeling inspired! Like I mentioned at the beginning, have a pen and paper close by all the time if you can. Ideas will appear at interesting times, especially when you are feeling happy, grateful, at ease, and calm. Your own unique ideas will come to you with ease and flow.

You can also let go of any preconceived ideas you have and completely clear your mind. Go into your creation with no thought of the outcome. Turn on some music and pick out some colours that you resonate with at the time. Pick up the paint brush, pencil, ink, whatever you are using, and just go for it, and just start creating! The medium you are using may guide you to articulate a really good idea along the way to create something amazing! Let everything flow and your creation may begin to look like something—like a flower, bird, jungle—who knows! That may lead you in a certain direction with the creation. So, to begin your creation, find a place to start, and once you get going, art may just surprise you! Add those different colours in there!

Things will happen that you never expect when you just completely let go.

Letting go of perfectionism really helps with coming up with your own ideas. It gives you that chance to let go and not worry about making mistakes or worry about being different. The focus instead is on doing what feels right.

Be bold and unique; standout from the crowd! Turn that blank canvas into a masterpiece that's 100% YOU! Ignite having your own ideas with ease and flow. Show people who you are and what you want to bring to the world. While doing this, let your incredible emotions shine. Let's talk about that next!

Incredible Emotions

Art is feeling; it's all about how it makes a person feel inside. When someone comes into contact with your artwork, think about the feeling you want to portray within your art. How would you like the viewer to feel when they see your art?

You can intentionally instill emotions within your artwork. The viewer will be able to feel these emotions just by looking at your artwork. That's when you know you've created something truly impactful!

You can instill emotions into your artwork by really utilizing your own emotions towards the artwork. If you want to create a calm feeling in your artwork for your viewers, you can turn on some calming music, relax, and/or meditate before you start to create. Basically just create a calm aura and calm space in your mind for you to be in at the time that you are creating your artwork. When you're feeling calm, generally, what you create will reflect that emotion!

Art is incredibly therapeutic, so it can also be used to push past anger, frustration, heartbreak, etc. I have done this in the past! Pablo Picasso quotes, *"The purpose of art is washing the dust of daily life off our souls."* I don't believe that that's the whole purpose of art, but it's true in some cases. When I was heartbroken, I would toss my whole heart and soul into a painting to get all of my emotions out. I have literally spent 5 days straight working on a painting, and just took breaks for the basic necessities in between, of course. Did it help? For me, yes it did! I was able to just let myself get all the emotions I was feeling, out of me, and turn them into an absolutely beautiful piece of artwork! I always feel so much better after doing that, too, because I know that I chose not to keep my emotions bottled up. We all know how unhealthy bottling things up and holding them in can be, so remember to let things go! Feel your emotions first, of course; it's okay to cry or be sad, because if we didn't experience sadness, how would we know what true happiness feels like, right?

After feeling your emotions, though, remember to pick yourself up and choose to let them go so that they don't linger with you and affect you in several negative ways in your future.

Holding on would only hurt you in the end, and your relationships with others. If you don't agree with what the person did, and you don't respect them for it, you can still choose to forgive them: "I don't condone what you did, but I forgive you!" Just saying that in your head and putting full meaning towards it can feel incredibly freeing and take a massive load off of your shoulders! Rather than feeling hate and displeasure every time something happens that reminds you of that person or situation, forgiving and letting go will put your own happiness first and truly set your soul free!

For life, something I've come to realize about emotions is that when you put meaning to something, it engraves it in your mind. I realized this with scary movies. When I watched a couple of scary movies as a child, an image of the scariest part of the movie would always stick in my mind, and I didn't like it one bit! I finally realized it was because of the meaning I put to that moment. I felt fearful emotions while I was watching it; that gave the scenes meaning, and my mind held onto those scenes. Even to this day, I can still picture the scenes in my head. It's important to stay neutral, be aware, and choose the meaning you place on something.

Another great point that kind of ties back in with being present in the moment, is if you're holding back what you truly want to say and show, it means you have a block from the past or a fear of the future. I know this kind of realization may be hard to understand at first, but it's true! You may be afraid of judgement and afraid to truly express yourself and your feelings.

Maybe you were told in the past, "Stop crying," "Why are you crying?" or, "Don't be a baby," and in those cases and many others, that might be what is blocking you from fully expressing who you are! Maybe you felt so ignored when you tried to express yourself so many times, that you just gave up. Maybe you have a past relationship that hurt your ego. Maybe someone laughed at you when you expressed who you are. Whatever it may be, you may be holding onto something like that from the past, and it's affecting how you communicate your emotions in your relationships and through your art!

So, how can you break down your wall and get past that? Be present in the moment right now! It's your ego getting in the way, making you fear judgement! Guess what, though? Your ego can only live in the past and future; it can't live in the present moment! So, if situations are coming up and you're choosing not to truly express your feelings, it means you are thinking from the past or future and letting those get in the way of the moment you're currently in. It's a big realization to have, and it truly changed my life! I caught myself in this tangle and was happy to know why I wasn't expressing myself to the fullest. If you focus on staying neutral (not being hard on yourself for it) and having kind intentions towards others (in the present moment right now), it becomes harder for the ego to push through that, and you will make it harder and harder for your ego to pop out, every single time you choose to be stronger than it.

If you see something special within a person, tell them! For you, it only takes 2 seconds to say, but for them, the meaning of those words could last a lifetime and make a huge impact in their life.

Choose to feel incredible emotions in life and be enthusiastic about your journey! Enjoy what you have at this very moment! Harness those beautiful emotions to level up and expand your experiences and creations!

Now that you feel all the feels and can express yourself in beautiful ways, it's time to be grateful for yourself.

Now Be Grateful for You

What does genuine gratitude feel like? It may feel different to everyone. For me, personally, it's a feeling of love, joy, wholeness, and thankfulness. It's an energy that flows through my entire being. It's almost like a tingle of warmth and happiness throughout my entire heart and soul!

Having gratitude is such an important part of life! Why is gratitude important? Appreciating what you have in this very moment creates a sense of wholeness within your heart. It gives you a sense and awareness of how truly blessed you are. The best part is that the more grateful you are, the more things you will attract to be grateful for.

Ignite being grateful for yourself! You are an incredible human being, and you deserve to be grateful for who you are and who you are becoming. You were born for a bigger reason than you probably realize. Step into your divine self!

Having a gratitude journal (any notebook will work) can be very beneficial to you if you choose to get one. It's a place to write out what and who you are grateful for: "I am so happy and grateful that…" and to write what you are grateful for in this moment! Feel the gratitude run through your soul. As American author Neville Goddard always says, *"Feeling is the secret!"* You can also be grateful for something that hasn't happened yet. You can be grateful in advance: "I am so happy and grateful now that…" and add what you are grateful for now that hasn't even happened in the physical world yet, but you know it's happening and coming. If you've ever heard of manifestation, you have probably already heard those gratitude lines, and know that they are very powerful!

Early in the morning when you wake up, or late at night before bed, or both, is the best time to write and feel gratitude. Anytime of the day is great, but in the morning, it sets the tone for your entire day; and at night, it puts you in such a beautiful state before sleeping, especially if you set an intention of your goal along with it so that it will soak into your subconscious mind during your sleep.

Pay attention to how you feel when you're in a grateful state, and embrace that feeling! Hold onto that feeling and make it part of you and part of your day-to-day life! Living in a grateful state will help you attract more things to be grateful for. Gratitude will also make a positive impression in your subconscious mind over time!

Even if you experience contrast (something isn't going as planned), give yourself grace and know that everything happens for a reason, and the reason is probably for you to grow! Have you ever heard the saying, "Blessings or lessons?" God gives you blessings or lessons in life, so if you experience contrast, it's okay; you're meant to learn and grow from it!

Also, be grateful for yourself at this very moment. You chose to read this book, and you're choosing to change the way you think and the way you want to be. Genuinely say thank you to yourself, always. You are truly amazing!

Pure happiness and gratitude are truly my go-to's when it comes to creating. It's a great way for you to set the tone in your mind to be in such a beautiful state of flow, to come up with your own ideas! Now you can develop or define your style!

Your Style

You've experimented and you have developed your own ideas, so now it's time to define your style! Your style is kind of when you find a way of creating that you truly love. It can be using certain colour tones, certain techniques, and/or certain art movements of creating. If you don't feel that you have a style yet, you will develop one along the way.

Some styles can include small brush strokes, large brush strokes, etc. What type of art do you create? Are you a landscape artist? Do you only paint flowers, while using small brush strokes? Do you draw cat photos in charcoal? Some styles can be very specific and turn into a niche. Is your art abstract, surrealism, pointillism, realism, etc.? There are several different styles/movements of art, so I recommend looking up photos on the internet for examples of what they look like, and to read about them so that you are able to define what style/movement your art typically fits in with, if it fits in with one. If your art doesn't fit in with a style/movement, that's okay too; it doesn't have to! Maybe you're a trailblazer and you're creating your own movement!

Someone said to me a long time ago, "You've got to develop a style now." I went home and looked at all of my original artwork on the wall and thought, "You know what, I already have a style!" The person may not have seen it at the time, but I could see my own unique style in my art. Others became aware of my style shortly after that too, probably because I believed in myself. When you get to a certain point of having created so many originals, your style will shine through and will be well known to the people around you, especially if you are showing off your creations along the way.

When you develop your style, you will know. When your audience continuously compliments you for something specific about your artwork, it will allow you to know what your strong point is. I always get compliments on my vibrant colours and inspiration. That's what people love most about my paintings, and that is definitely my style! It's what I love to create and what I am incredible at creating! When your audience sees your art next to another piece of art, and they know which one's yours automatically, that's when you know you have a style! Pay attention to people's feedback, because it may help you to realize that you have a style that you may not have known was already there.

It feels incredible to be able to say you have a style, and for people to just know when they see a (insert your full name or artist name here) _____ original! Now that you've developed a style, it's important to see all of the opportunities being presented to you while you create.

Opportunities

Has your paintbrush, pen, or anything else ever slipped into the wrong spot? Has your hand smudged the colour you just put on the page/canvas? Well, let's just say it happens to the best of us! I used to get upset when this would happen, and I wouldn't know what to do. There was so much frustration! When this happens to you, learn to give yourself some grace. I personally first try to wipe off the "mistake" to see if it will easily come off. It's worth a shot, right? If that doesn't work, I choose to see the so-called "mistake" as a beautiful opportunity.

I know you're probably wondering, how on Earth is a "mistake" a beautiful opportunity? The truth is, all it takes is a change in mindset, a different perception of it! See the opportunity that is being presented to you. It's like American painter Bob Ross always said, *"A happy little accident."* I personally choose to believe that there's always a way to fix a creation. You can choose to believe the same.

Just think of all the possibilities of what you can do with the smudge that your hand or artistic tool of choice created. Maybe it's telling you that something else is meant to be there. Make it your mission to turn the smudge into something beautiful, and incorporate it as part of the artwork! You can literally do that; you can make the smudge look like it was intentionally placed in that spot, and make it look in harmony with the rest of your artwork!

If the "mistake" is kind of an "out of the line" situation, where you smudged out of the lines of the object you were creating, that can easily be fixed by extending the image you are creating outwards a little bit. It's so simple and works like a charm! Other times, you may have an opportunity to add something different to the artwork. Just think, "Hmm, what can I add here? Maybe I'll add an extra leaf, a bird, a cloud, a rock, a swirl." The possibilities are truly endless and infinite! You can add whatever you decide fits your creation, to keep it harmonious and true to the concept you are creating.

Let me tell you, every time I make a "mistake," my artwork turns out way better than it would have in the first place! It kind of gives you that chance to add something different that you may not have thought of or added if you didn't accidently make that smudge.

Seeing a "mistake" as an opportunity will allow you to dig deeper and really pull ideas from your imagination. Understand that everything happens for a reason and, generally, the reason is for your highest good. Even if you don't see the reason right away, it will eventually shine, and you will understand why that happened. I truly believe that everything happens for a reason, with every bit of my heart and soul!

All in all, if you make a "mistake" on your creation and see it as a dead-end point, then the only thing stopping you from succeeding is you! Get out of your own way! I challenge you to expand your consciousness and choose to always see a "mistake" as the most amazing opportunity being presented to you. There are so many options to elevate your creation from that point on!

Now that you choose to see opportunities, it's time to hold unwavering faith! Why? Find out right now!

Unwavering Faith

By now you've probably developed more confidence in yourself. Remember to trust yourself; YOU are confident!

Let's get right into it. What is faith? Faith is complete, wholehearted trust or confidence in something or someone. It's also defined as having a strong belief in God. Faith, to me personally, is trusting in yourself, and trusting in God to guide you on your journey by working through you! It's listening to your heart, to allow your intuition to guide you (God working through you). It's knowing with your entire heart and soul that everything will work out in your highest good!

So why is faith so important? Well, firstly, if you don't trust in yourself, who will? Trust comes from within first! Develop wholehearted trust within yourself. Author and political activist Helen Keller once said, *"What I am looking for is not out there; it is in me."* Everything you need is already within you; you just have to have the faith and know that it's there! Utilize what you have within you and utilize what's right in front of you.

Faith connects you with a higher being; in my belief, it's God. It helps to connect you with the oneness of the world. We are all one, and we are all connected. We are spiritual beings in physical bodies. When you are connected, you will allow God to work through you.

Faith is believing in the unseen. Like we talked about before, create the life you want within your imagination. Anything you can see is real! As the late Bob Proctor (expert in law of attraction, speaker, author, etc.) would always say, *"Believing in the unseen is a triumph and a blessing."* It truly is! Anything backed up by unwavering faith, turns what seems to be the impossible, into the possible!

We all had so much faith when we were children! If our parents told us something like, "We're moving," we didn't question if it was a lie. We had no doubts about our parents. We believed them and carried on with our day with full belief and trust that what they told us was going to happen. Believe in yourself like you believed things as a child—full, wholehearted belief! Have unwavering faith where no one can convince you otherwise.

One thing you may be thinking is, "Is faith a form of hoping?" The answer is no. If you are hoping something will happen, it means that you don't have wholehearted faith and know that it will happen; it means you have a wish that something will happen! Don't get me wrong; hope still has its place in the world, but it just differs from having true and unwavering faith.

Have faith that you will succeed. You may have doubts and think, "Well, I don't want to set my expectations too high and then get disappointed." My answer to that is to always expect success. Let go of the doubt and fear in your mind and choose faith! Faith and fear both involve believing in the unseen, and they both involve the same amount of effort. Which one will you choose? I'm personally going to choose to have faith, always, and expect the best for myself to attract the best!

Just when you think something is impossible, if you hold wholehearted belief and unwavering faith that what you want to happen will happen, God will rearrange events and people in the Universe to make it happen! Trust me, I've seen this and also heard of this happening a lot. You will manifest what it is that you want into physical form.

Always look at your truth. YOU are a creator, an artist, of your life and canvas. Embody the divine artist that's already within you! YOU are absolutely incredible and will do amazing things in this world! Commit yourself to your goals and shoot for the stars! Remember, you're already a star. Everything you need is already within you; you just need to become aware of it. You've got this! It's just the beginning…

CHAPTER 6

A Few Final Thoughts

"What I am looking for is not out there; it is in me."
– Author and political activist, Helen Keller

Did You See What I Did There?

Take a look at the 4 I's in the table of contents at the front of the book. As you can see, the first letter of each bullet within the 4 I's chapters spell out, "Embody the Divine Artist Within YOU."

You already know you're the divine artist of your canvas and life, and now you can fully embody that title. YOU are empowered! Say it out loud, and be proud: "I am powerful, I am worthy, I am brave, I am bold, I am confident, I am grateful, I am creative, I am empowered, I am my divine self and a divine artist!" Ultimately, be the incredible artist you're destined to be. Everything you need has been within you this whole time; you just may not have realized it until now. You are the creator of your life and your artwork! Choose to make them both extraordinary!

Life's about filling your cup! Feel fulfilled and live an abundant life by living your purpose every single day—that's how to fill your cup!

Now I'd love to give you a huge congratulations!

For bonuses go to www.empoweredcreatorbook.com

Congratulations!

CONGRATULATIONS! You made it to the other side! You did it! YOU are an empowered creator! I am so proud of you!

You are worthy! You are imaginative! You are inspired! You are confident! You are brave and courageous! You are bold! You are authentic and unique! You are the most incredible artist of your canvas and your life! I'm so proud and happy for you, and I'm so grateful to be a part of your journey! Happy creating!

Next is a list of golden nuggets from the book. I chose this list specifically to have really important points I've mentioned within the book, and some "Aha" moments that I've had on my journey as an artist, which I feel will be most helpful to you. I am leaving some pages blank so that you can add your own big takeaways as well—your own gold nuggets!

Gold Nuggets Recap

Here is a list of my favourite gold nuggets from within the book! Please feel free to add your biggest gold nugget takeaways on the blank pages after these.

Take an honest look at yourself. When I say an honest look, I don't mean with judgement or disappointment; I mean staying neutral but taking an honest look to see the areas in your life where you can grow and expand yourself.

Imagination is one of your higher faculties of thinking. It is forming new concepts, ideas, and images in your mind without the input of your 5 senses. These mental images are not something you can hear, taste, touch, or see physically with your eyes, but you can see them in your mind and imagine their realness. Imagination is inventing something new.

Imagination is like a muscle. Keep using it and it will continue to expand and grow. Build the muscle of your imagination. The more you use it, the more ideas will flow to you regularly!

Be mindful of what you are creating with your imagination; try to be consciously aware and monitor your thoughts. Use your imagination for good, to make your life more fulfilling and to make the world a better place!

Ideas and concepts will come to you effortlessly if you stay open to receive them! They will appear at interesting times, especially when you are feeling happy, grateful, at ease, and calm.

Inspiration is EVERYWHERE! It can be found in nature, in books, in colours, in absolutely anything you see or do!

An inspired thought feels like that "Aha" moment, where an idea strikes you and you feel that "whoa" feeling inside, and you run to find a piece of paper to write down your idea as fast as possible!

Focus on what's right in front of you, right at this very moment! Being present and valuing those moments is so important to feel inspired, and to just live a fulfilling and happy life in general. Be in a place of just being. It's amazing how calm and content you will feel!

One inspired thought will lead to the next!

Open the floodgates of your imagination! When you are in a state of flow, the way will seem effortless… the "effortless way." The effortless way is when you're moving in the right direction with so much ease and flow. It's allowing God to show you the path of least resistance!

Choose to think outside the box, and don't be afraid to be unconventional! Think of the extraordinary, where anything is possible and anything goes. The only limitation is something like the law of gravity. We know it's exact every single time!

Start paying attention to the way you speak to yourself. Choose to be the best version of yourself that you can be, from now on. Speak as kindly to yourself as you would to others!

Intuition is the ability to understand something instantly without the need for reasoning. You just know! It's your awareness of that gut feeling within you that's telling you to do something or to not do something. It's basically an instinctive feeling instead of conscious reasoning. It's when you follow your heart and let God work through you!

Not everything has to have a reason beforehand. When something feels right within your heart, do that! I know you may like to analyze things and reason ahead of time before making decisions, but it's time to put your analytical mind aside for once. For the decisions you make in life, your heart will know what you truly want if you choose to listen to it.

Stop living the way everyone expects you to live and, instead, live the way YOU truly want to live. It takes courage and bravery to do this. Choose to shine your uniqueness to the world!

People's opinions of you are none of your business!

For bonuses go to ...

See yourself as someone who is growing every single day. Focus on being 1% better and moving 1% closer to your goal by taking imperfect action.

Know your creation is complete when it feels good and makes you feel whole and happy inside, and your heart is telling you to stop. Another way to tell when a creation is done is when you've captured exactly what you wanted to capture, within your creation, like a concept or idea.

It's time to step into being the person you truly want to be, and to embody that new identity! Embody the person you want to become before becoming him/her! This will close the gap faster, and you will become who you're truly meant to be, in a quantum leap!

There is a risk involved in everything, so you will be taking a risk regardless. Choose your risk wisely; bet on yourself for once!

Use autosuggestion and "I am…" affirmations to build belief in yourself. In the meantime, believe that I believe in you!

In his book, *You^2,* Price Pritchett, PH.D., said, *"You know more than you know you know!"*

Be bold and unique; standout from the crowd! Turn that blank canvas into a masterpiece that's 100% YOU!

Add your personality and your vibrations to your creations.

Art is feeling; it's all about how it makes a person feel inside. Think about the feeling you want to portray within your art. You can intentionally instill emotions within your artwork. The viewer will be able to feel these emotions just by looking at your artwork. You've created something truly impactful!

The more grateful you are for what you have in life, the more things you will attract to be grateful for!

Don't over-think it!

Make bravery so strong that fear is obsolete and just disintegrates because you're no longer focusing on it. There will only be room for bravery and boldness!

Your ego can only live in the past and future; it can't live in the present moment. Be present in the moment right now!

Seeing a "mistake" as an opportunity will allow you to dig deeper and really pull ideas from your imagination. Understand that everything happens for a reason and, generally, the reason is for your highest good!

The only thing stopping you from succeeding is you! Get out of your own way!

For bonuses go to www.empoweredcreatorbook.com

Faith and fear both involve believing in the unseen, and they both involve the same amount of effort. Choose to have unwavering faith that God is working through you, and trust that everything is happening for your highest good!

You are worthy! You are imaginative! You are inspired! You are confident! You are brave and courageous! You are bold! You are authentic and unique! YOU are the most incredible artist of your canvas and your life!

Your Gold Nuggets

For bonuses go to ...

Your Gold Nuggets

www.EmpoweredCreatorBook.com

Your Gold Nuggets

For bonuses go to www.EmpoweredCreatorBook.com

Your Gold Nuggets

RESOURCES

*I*f you'd love to have more colour, inspiration, and joy in your life, please check out my websites and social media for more support and empowerment!

WEBSITES:
To receive the bonuses, and to see the coloured images of my original paintings that are shown on the title pages throughout the book, check out:

www.EmpoweredCreatorBook.com
www.KatySpeziale.com

SOCIAL MEDIA:
Instagram –https://www.instagram.com/katyspezialeart/
Facebook –https://www.facebook.com/katyspezialeart

YOUTUBE:
YouTube –https://www.youtube.com/channel/UCNzK4EJbvqCcI8kSPuLqWYg/featured

ABOUT THE AUTHOR

Meet Katy

Katy is an artist, award-winning author, imagination catalyst, creativity cultivator, mentor, celiac enthusiast, and foodie.

It's her mission to empower people to embody colourful and easy lives so that they will live with joy and inspiration.

Being from a small town in Northern Ontario, Katy has thoroughly enjoyed writing stories and using her imagination to the fullest since she was a child.

As a painter and a writer, when she entered into the personal development world, she realized everything that she had overcome as an artist.

Now Katy strives to help other artists overcome these challenges (perfectionism, coming up with their own ideas, self-image, etc.) as well!

For bonuses go to www.EmpoweredCreatorBook.com

She wants to empower artists to bring out the bravery, boldness, and confidence within them, so that they will see their worth and the potential that's already within them.

Katy understands that we all have beautiful gifts to bring to the world, which we should be sharing with our entire hearts and souls!

Her style has developed so much over the years and is so pronounced in all of her artwork, and now it's her mission to inspire artists to discover their styles and discover their divine selves.

You can discover more of her work here:
www.KatySpeziale.com